THE

MYSTERIES AND MISERIES

OF

New York:

A STORY OF REAL LIFE,

BY NED BUNTLINE.

PART V.

NEW YORK:
EDWARD Z. C. JUDSON.
1848.

PART FIVE.

CHAPTER I.

GUSTAVE LIVINGSTON waited some time in the saloon of Madam P. expecting Charles Meadows to come up, but at last he became impatient, and having swallowed the beverage which that very respectable elderly lady had concocted for him, and paid her for the same, he hurried down into the street to seek his companion.

But he was no where in sight.

"Cursed uncivil!" muttered Gus. "especially when I'd ordered liquor for him! I wonder where he can have gone too?"

The reader probably will feel the same curiosity.

When Charles had turned to speak with Carlton, the latter drew him over to the opposite side of the street and in a low tone said:

"I am now arranging that business for you! You must manage to get excused from the store to-day—I wish you to spend the day with me!"

"I cannot," replied the clerk, with a shudder—"I have several important accounts to make out for Mr. S."

"They *must* be deferred until to-morrow!" said Carlton, in a firm tone. "This day must be spent with me—for we have weighty matters to arrange!"

"Relative to my leaving the city?"

"Yes," replied the gambler, "and also in the other matter which formed the subject of our last conversation!"

"The murder?—Oh, for God's sake spare me from that!" gasped Meadows, with a shudder.

"Pshaw, don't be a fool, young man!" replied the other,

grating his teeth in his impatience. "I thought this was all settled between us!"

"So it was—yet it is dreadful to do a murder!" replied Meadows, keeping his eyes fixed upon the ground as if he did not dare to lift them, even to the face of the wretch who confronted him.

"It's nothing after you get used to it!" replied the gambler, in a careless tone. "If I was not sure to be suspected, I'd kill the rascal, myself! I'd no more mind putting him out of the way, than I would a snake that lay in my path!"

"The dream will come true—and if *one*, the other!" muttered Meadows, not seeming to heed the remarks of Carlton.

"What dream are you talking of?" asked the latter.

"You know Harry Whitmore!" continued Meadows, without heeding the question—"What kind of a man is he?"

"A devilish *fine* fellow!" replied Carlton.

"But is he honorable—is he not a *libertine?*" continued the clerk, raising his eyes in a searching glance to the face of the other.

"A libertine? No, indeed! Harry may sometimes cruise around a little and go to *see* the fashions, but he was never wild in that way, to my knowledge!"

"You do not believe he would ruin a pure young girl under the mask of love and friendship?"

"No, indeed! He would be the last man in the world to do that! He is the very soul of honor!" replied the gambler, who, though he did not comprehend the reason or drift of the clerk's questionings, knew enough to protect the "fair name" of a confederate in villainy.

Meadows seemed to breathe more freely after Carlton's last reply. A load was taken from his breast.

"I will not believe the dream in regard to *her*," he murmured, "but *mine* must come true!"

"What dreams are you speaking of?" cried Carlton. "Blast the thing—you must be crazy!"

"No, not yet!" replied Meadows, "but I've a very fair prospect of being so before long!"

"Pshaw, man! you are acting childishly. Go to your store

and excuse yourself—tell them your mother is very sick, or use some other white fib, and then come to my rooms. We will arrange our matters over a quiet glass of that old Osborn wine !"

"Does *he* know anything of it ?" asked Meadows, indicating with a gesture, Sam. Selden, who stood on the opposite curbstone tapping the toe of his elegant boot with a slight rattan held in his gloved hand.

"Yes, Sam. and me have no secrets between us !" said Carlton.

The gambler was slightly mistaken. He did not know that Selden had tried first to seduce his wife—and that if he had succeeded, he would have been the last to excite her husband's jealousy.

"Why could not he do this job ?" asked the clerk.

"Because, as I told you before, he and I are too intimate. He, like myself, would be suspected. When the deed is done we must *both* be at home. You will not even be dreamed of !"

"Ha ! ha ! I have been already !" cried Meadows, with a hollow laugh.

"What ! why young man you must be crazy ? What do you mean ?"

"My mother dreamed that she saw me kill a man last night !"

"Indeed ! well her dream will come true—but old women's dreams are not evidence in law now-a-days. You'll be in no danger from her evidence or anything else !"

"I wish it was all over !" sighed the unhappy young man, "and that I and my family were across the blue waters !"

"So do I, heartily," added Carlton, "but if wishes were horses beggars might ride. You must *act ;* it lies with yourself to finish all and to be off in less than a week !"

"Yes, and it must be done !" said the clerk, gloomily. "You must *arrange* all—I am but your tool, and you can use me !"

"Well, you'll get excused and spend the day with me ?"

"Yes, if I must !"

"Very well, then. We'll separate now—it is not best for us to be seen together much. I'll expect you in half an hour !"

Carlton rejoined Selden and passed on up the street, while Meadows with his eyes still fixed upon the ground turned the

corner and walked down Broadway, entirely forgetting Gus.
Livingston who waited for him in Madam P.'s saloon.

"Cursed uncivil!" said the latter when he came down and
found that Meadows had gone away. "But these clerks never
can learn *our* ways! I'll go and attend to Harry's business.
I wonder if I can't get a peep at the girl? If Harry wasn't my
friend now, I'd—— but no I'll not think of that. I wonder what
has become of the little sewing girl. She was a sweet minx—
it was foolish in her and her mother to run away from me—
they could have made more out of me than they can earn by
sewing!"

While thus soliloquising, Livingston was walking down toward Church street, on his way to the den where poor Isabella
was still confined.

She had not closed her eyes during the long and weary night.
She had listened to the rough shoutings of drunken men in
the streets—she had heard the tolling of the fire-bell—she had
heard the old clock of St. John's tell each hour as it rolled slowly
along over the heavy ocean of time. She had shuddered while
she listened to the sounds of revelry in the rooms below—and
she had heard shrieks mingling with laughter. It was a dreadful night to her. And yet the poor girl who had been sent in to
pass the night with her, glad of a chance to get one night's rest,
slept—slept as soundly as if guilt and misery had not made
their home in her bosom.

Daylight came, and through the slatted blinds of the fastened
shutters, thin rays of early light peeped in. Isabella once more
tried the small window, but it was closely fastened; besides, it
was so small that her body could scarcely have passed through
it, if it were open.

"No hope—not even of death!" she murmured, tearfully.
"Oh! if my brother or my poor mother knew of this! Charles
would rescue me, or die!"

At that very moment they were talking of her, for it was the
time when Mrs. Meadows was relating her dream.

The sun came up above the ridges of the houses which arose
to the eastward of her garret, and faint streaks of its glittering
light came into the room. One ray fell upon the Bible which

he had laid down again upon the table, as if it would point to er that there was her only hope and consolation.

At this moment the girl, who had slept so soundly, woke, rith a start, and looking wildly around her, burst into tears.

"Oh, dear!" she murmured, "I had such a happy dream. I iought I was at home again, sleeping in the little back room rith my sister Lottie, and the flowers were twining up around ie window casings; and I heard the birds sing just as I used to o! Oh, why could I not have died in such a dream!"

"Poor girl!" sighed Isabella; "death would indeed be a re- ef from such a life; yet you do not wish to die!"

"No, no, not exactly! I do wonder if it's breakfast time!" plied the girl, recovering from the momentary delirium of her eam, and sinking its "romance" into plain "reality."

"Has no one been in yet?" she continued.

"No," replied Isabella; "since about three o'clock everything is been still in the house!"

"Yes; that's shuttin' up hour!" said the girl; "but you didn't idress—haven't you been to bed?"

"No," replied Isabella; "I have not closed my eyes—nor will except in death, while I remain under this roof!"

"You oughtn't to take on so!" said the girl—"it's no use. re seen others act just so, and they didn't make nothin' by it! ertrude did just so, till they starved her into the ways, and en, after all, she cried herself a'most to death!"

"No wonder; if tears will kill one, then I shall soon die!" ;hed Isabella.

"Don't talk of dying! It's a great deal better to live!" said e gírl, forgetting her own expression upon awakening.

Their conversation was interrupted by some one opening the or. The next moment a hideous-looking, poc-marked old ;gro woman opened the door, and said to the young girl:

"Missus wants you, Miss Clementina!"

"Is that your name?" asked Isabella, of the young girl.

"It's the name Ma'am S. gave me, but my real name is ary," replied the girl. "All the girls have new names given 'em when they come here. We've got a Fanny Ellsler—a

Virginie—a Lady Montague—a Blanche and Constance—but they're all fancy names !"

"Missus wants you right away, Miss Clem. !" cried the old negress, and then dropping a curtsy, while she grinned a horrible attempt at a smile, she looked at Isabella and said :

"If de new Missee please—Joanner 'll take her footin'.!"

"Isabella glanced at her companion to know the meaning of this strange remark.

"She means you must give her a present. It's always the way when girls first come out !"

"Alas ! I have nothing in the world to give her, here ; but if she or you will help me out of this dreadful house, I'll give you all that I can get ! *Do,* if you have hearts in you—*do* help me away from here. Just let me out !"

"I'd like to see 'em do it !" said a sharp voice at the door, and the flushed face of Ma'am S. was thrust in.

"Clem., go down stairs !" said she. "Joanna, go and attend to your cooking ! when I send you on an errand, I want you to hurry ; not to stop and palaver with my boarders !"

The negress and the young girl vanished before this storm of words, and the landlady stood alone in the door-way, with her arms akimbo, and her hands resting upon her hips.

"Young lady," said she, in a lower tone, " if you know what is best for you, you'll just take things easy. No one is agoin' to hurt you—and if you'll only be quiet, I'll treat you like a lady. Anything you want to eat or drink shall be sent up—you shall have books, or the papers, or anything that's reasonable !"

"Oh, for mercy's sake, then, let me go home !"

"That's unreasonable !" replied the landlady. "Your lover, Harry Whitmore, has engaged board for you—and as he pays me a hundred dollars a week it would be a losing business for me to part with you !"

"Oh, God, have mercy on me ! Is there no hope !" murmured the unhappy girl, while tears burst afresh from her swollen eyes.

"There's no use in your taking on about it !" said the woman, coldly. "Your betters have led the way before you. It's only your fancy and rotted pride that makes you fret. Harry 'll keep you like a lady, if you behave yourself, and if you don't choose to take it easy, you may take it rough, that's all!"

"Oh, mercy! mercy! If you'll let me go from here I'll give you a hundred, yes, five hundred dollars!"

"Poh! Harry would give me a thousand to keep you. You must think I'm green! Just make yourself easy, my lady, that's my advice. Now be a good girl and I'll be a mother to you!"

"A mother? Oh, God, if my mother only knew where I was!" sighed the wretched girl.

"Yes, but the *if* is in the way!" said the hag. She was about to say more, but hearing the bell of the street door rung, she locked the door upon Isabella, and descended. She found Gus. Livingston at the door, whom, as a friend and follower of Whitmore, she knew very well.

"Well, Gus.," said she, familiarly, "what brings you here so early. I didn't know that you was brave enough to come to my door in the open day-light!"

"Business makes a difference!" said Gus., as he entered the open door.

"Yes, *in* course, but what *is* your business?" asked the landlady.

"You've got a bird here caged for Harry Whitmore!"

"Yes, I s'pose he told you so!"

"Yes, and sent me here to pay his respects, as he is unable to come, and also to pay you over a couple of hundred!" said Gus., handing her the money.

"Why, what's the matter with him this morning!" asked the landlady—"did he go on a spree last night—headache and all that, this morning?"

"Well, his head certainly must ache a little, there being a lump on it fully as large as a piece of chalk—but a broken arm is his main excuse for sending a substitute this morning!"

"Why, you don't mean to say he has given the girl over to you?" exclaimed Ma'am S.

"No, not exactly. But he told me to see the young fool, and talk to her!"

"Well, you won't make much at it. She's all clouds and rain-drops. It is strange what fools these young girls *are*, but they *will* be so, there isn't one in five hundred that takes to living out naturally !"

"Where is she ?" asked Livingston, who, in attempting to see Isabella, was certainly overstepping the errand upon which he came.

"Up stairs; I'll show you her room—but you mus'n't offer to plague her !" replied the landlady.

"Of course not—I'm Harry's *friend* and *honor*, you know !" replied Gus.

"There's devellish little honor amongst men where a pretty girl's in the way !" replied Ma'am S., evincing a very true knowledge of human nature in her remark. "But I'll trust you, Gus.," she added—"because you know that Harry would cut your heart out if you was to try to take her away from him !"

"He isn't in a way to do much cutting just now !" said Gus. with a laugh, following the landlady up stairs.

"When'll he be able to be out—you didn't tell me now his arm was broken !" said Ma'am S.

"Answering your last question first—he got his arm broken in a row—and he'll not be out for a day or two yet !"

"Well, so much the better. The girl 'll have time to settle down and be reasonable !" said the landlady.

The next moment she unlocked the door, and Gus. Livingston stood in the presence of Isabella. Ma'am S. retired at the same time.

"Miss Meadows, I presume ?" said Livingston. "We have met before, I believe !"

Isabella could not for a moment bring him to her recollection, for he was dressed in the height of fashion, and looked quite differently from his appearance when dressed in a priest's gown.

"Have you too come here to persecute me ?" she asked, sadly, as she shrunk back from his earnest gaze.

"No, indeed, my dear Miss ; quite the contrary, I assure you, upon my honor. Knowing your brother as intimately as I do, I cannot be otherwise than a *friend !*"

"A friend !" she cried—"yet you are *his*, Henry Whitmore's friend ! I remember you now—I saw you last night—your dress only was different !"

"It is very true, Miss Meadows, and I was performing my part in a little masquerade got up by my friend Whitmore, but I did not dream that *you* were intended for a part in it !"

"Then you were not a willing accomplice in his villainy ?" asked the trembling girl.

"*Indeed* I was not—I did not know that *you* were there, or that Harry had any dishonorable intentions toward you. If I had, I should not have permitted it; my regard for my particular friend, your brother, whom I saw but a few minutes ago, would have forbidden it !"

"You saw him, you say, a few minutes ago—did you tell him of my situation ?"

"No," replied Livingston, "I thought it best to rescue you from it without a noise; it will preserve your reputation, you know, from any little remarks which might be made !"

"Then you have come here to rescue me ?"

"Not exactly to take you away from here at this moment, but to prepare you for it !" replied Gus.

"I do not understand you !" said Isabella.

"I'll try to explain, if you will be seated. Do not fear me !" replied Gus., taking a seat himself. "I am indeed your friend, or I should not be here !"

"I must trust you,—but oh, for God's sake do not deceive me !" said Isabella, taking the chair which he pushed toward her.

"Honor, Miss Meadows, honor will prevent it," replied the young man, drawing his chair close to her side. "I will now tell you all. Whitmore is laid up in bed—he was very seriously injured in a fight last night !"

"Thank God !" murmured Isabella—"but it was not with my brother ?"

"Oh, no, he parted with your brother on very excellent terms, about midnight, but got into a difficulty soon afterwards, and had several bones broken !"

"Thank God ! then I am safe from his persecutions for the present, at least !" sighed the unhappy girl. "But why cannot I at once go home—will you not take me from here ?"

"You would not leave a house like this in daylight, would you ?" asked Gus., apparently surprised.

"Yes, oh, do let me go at once. The very air is poison to me. Do take me home at once!"

"I am sorry, but I came here to arrange matters, so that Harry should be seen and forgiven, before you went away!" said Gus.

"Oh, I will forgive him, if I can leave here safely, but I do not want to see him!" cried Isabella.

"Not to forgive him?"

"No, for nothing. If you *are* my friend, *prove* it, call a carriage, and take me home!"

"But just think, Miss Meadows, if you were seen going out of this house with me in the day-time, it would ruin your reputation!"

"Not when all is known—oh, do not keep me here till night!"

"My regard for your reputation, and my duty as your brother's *friend*, will force me to do it, even at the risk of your displeasure!" said Gus., in a kind tone.

"Then will you promise to take me away as soon as it is dark?"

"Yes, on conditions!" replied the young man.

"What are they?" asked Isabella, in a tremulous tone.

Gus. took her by the hand gently, and in a manner as mild as if he were about to pay her a compliment, said—— Reader we cannot repeat his words. They were enough to bring the red blood up into her pale face with a mantling wave of fire—her large eyes flashed—she sprung to her feet, and while her beautiful form seemed to swell into an increased stature, she flung his hand from her, and shrieked, rather than spoke:

"Wretch! fiend! *dog!* Is this your friendship?"

"By Jove, you *are* a beauty!" cried Gus., looking upon her as she stood there in the very majesty of just anger, "I'll have a kiss if I die for it!"

As he spoke, he stepped toward her.

"Back, sir! stand back, if you value your life!" cried the indignant girl, forgetting that she was weak and weaponless.

"By Jove, but you do up tragedy well! Simpson would save the Park, if he'd engage you!" said Gus., still advancing.

She saw that she could not stop him, and bounding toward

the little window, dashed her form against it with her full force, crushing the glass, and endeavoring to precipitate herself through it into the street.

. She would inevitably have succeeded, had not Livingston seized her, and drawn her back. At the same moment Ma'am S. rushed into the room.

"What the deuce is the matter!" she cried. "What's all this, Gus. have you broken your word?"

"No, not exactly. I just tried to get a kiss from this proud chit, and she boxed my ears, and then tried to jump out of the window!"

"The more foolish she—but just come away, and let her alone!" said the landlady.

Gus. who was not much encouraged by his reception, complied with her request, and Isabella was once more alone.

She had cut her hand badly with the broken glass, but she did not speak or murmur. Her tears were dried—her face was pale—pale with desperation. Her compressed lips—flashing eyes and heaving bosom, all spoke of the same feeling. When the door was locked again, she returned to the window and examined it. A smile came over her pale face when she saw that she had loosened the casement, and now could push the shutter open.

"I can *die* now, when death or dishonor becomes my choice," she murmured, as she looked down from the dizzy height upon the ragged pavement below. And she smiled again at the thought, for she did not feel as defenceless as before.

Then she noticed that persons were continually passing to and fro below her, and a new thought rushed into her head, for when people are in peril, they think strangely fast.

She turned around to the table to seek for writing materials, but none were there. Yet her blood was streaming—it was a fitting ink to write a message of distress with. Tearing a blank leaf from a book, and taking a pin from her dress, she dipped the head of the latter in a gash in her hand, and wrote these words upon the paper.

"I am kept here a prisoner, against my will. For the love

of Heaven, come to my aid and rescue me while I am yet pure
and innocent, or send the police to my aid! God will reward
you, and a wretched, helpless girl will pray for you. I write in
my own blood—I have no ink!"

Quickly folding up this note, she returned to the window,
opened it a little way and peeped out.

She saw some negroes passing, but they looked ragged and
filthy, and she did not want to trust them.

A butcher's cart was approaching, and on its front a young,
red-headed, fair-faced fellow of twenty years of age, or there-
about, was seated. She saw only that he looked *honest*, and
that his eyes chanced to be turned up toward her face. She
reached out her hand and dropped the paper, and she could
have wept with joy when she saw that it fell into his cart. The
young man reached back and took it up, and then she saw him
check his horse and read the paper.

He did not seem exactly to understand it, for he scratched his
head and pored over it several minutes, and then looked back
at the window.

Isabella stretched out her bleeding hand, and watched his
motions with intense interest. But she could not tell what were
his intentions—for after again looking intently at the note, and
then turning his eyes toward her, he drove on up the street,
scratching his head as if search of an unexploded idea.

Now her heart was heaved upon the waves of uncertainty.
The question to her was whether he would return with help—
or let it pass by unheeded.

But into no better hands could her note have fallen, than into
those of red-headed Mose, the Bowery butcher-boy, one who
with some faults possessed some of the most sterling virtues that
ever warmed the human heart. His character in abler hands
than ours* has lately been held up before the world; and there-

* Mr. B. A. Baker, in two very spirited and life-like pieces, now playing with
astonishing success at the Olympic and Chatham Theatres in this city, has introduced the character of Mose, which is drawn from *life*, and it is played by CHAN-
FRAU as no man living but he, can play it. We are ever glad to see true talent
appreciated and rewarded, and the people seem certainly determined to reward
Messrs. Baker and Chanfrau, for they crowd nightly to see their pieces. Several
other characters familiar to our readers are to be seen in the play at the Chatham
We need not wish the author and actor success—they deserve and have it!

fore we will only say that though in an humble walk of life, Mose was every inch a *man!*

When he picked up the note, as we have already seen, he drove on a little ways and stopped to read it.

"This smells o' blood—by thunder!" he muttered, as he looked at it. "G'hal—prisoner 'g'inst her will! somethin's up—"

He paused and looked back at the little window, where he saw her white hand streaked with blood waving to him.

"Shouldn't wonder if there's a muss in that ere house to night!" muttered he, scratching his head, and again reading the hastily written note.

"She must be game!" he continued—"She aint afraid o' blood; she must be a gallo's g'hal. "I'll see her out—sure's my name's *Mose!* Can't do it now—must sarve the cust'mers and hunt up *Sikesey*, and four or five more of the b'hoys, and then it'll be dark and we can *go in*—we can!"

Mose took one more look at the window, and then putting the note away in a greasy pocket, beneath his white apron, amongst the proceeds of his morning's sales, was about to drive on, when Isabella put her head entirely out of the window.

Mose looked at her steadily for a moment.

"By gosh!" he muttered, "she looks *prezacly* like little 'Bell Meadows, sister to Charley, that I used to go to school with! It must be *her.* I'll go to look for Charley, soon's I get through my route!"

He determined to satisfy himself as to her identity, and turning his cart around, drove back past the house.

"Isn't that 'Bell Meadows?" he asked, in a low tone, but loud enough for her to hear it.

"Yes, yes! oh, do for Heaven's sake help me!" replied she.

"I won't do nothin' else—but you jist keep shady, and don't say nothin' to nobody afore night-time!" I'll be thar, *then*, me and Sikesey! But where's Charley?"

"In S——'s store. Oh, do let him know I'm locked up here!"

"Well, *I* will!" replied Mose, and then drove off.

CHAPTER II.

———

ANOTHER morning had dawned upon poor Angelina. Its light did not fall upon her flushed cheeks this time. Her fever had passed away, and there she lay, pale, weak and helpless, with scarce strength to speak.

Mr. Precise was nearly as pale as she, for he also had passed another sleepless night by her bed-side. He seemed to be as much interested in her fate, as if she was his own daughter, and tears welled out from his eyes as he noted how sadly fast she was changing.

It was not long after day-light that Jenny came up stairs, treading very noiselessly as he had directed her, and asked him if he would not go down to breakfast.

"No, Jenny—bring me a cup of tea, and a piece of toast, with a very little butter on it!" he replied; "and do the toast quite brown, Jenny!"

"Anything for her, poor thing?" asked Jenny, glancing at Angelina.

"No, not before the doctor comes. He said she musn't take anything till he saw her—he'll be here directly!" replied the kind old gentleman. Then, as Jenny was about to turn away, he asked:

"Where is Francis?"

"In the basement, readin' July Sneezer!" replied the maid.

"Reading what?" asked the old gentleman, in the same low tone.

"July Sneezer, out o' Shakspeare!" repeated the girl.

"Julius Cæsar, you mean, don't you, child?"

"Yes, sir, I s'pect that's it—it's very grand, he was just a readin' that part where Brutus sticks him in the stomach with a knife,—oh, it's so grand!"

"Well, well, never mind! Don't speak so loud, Jenny, you'll

disturb her. When you go down, tell Francis I want to see him, after he's had breakfast!"

The maid departed to enjoy more tragedy with her lover, or rather to take her part in the familiar and pleasant domestic drama of the Breakfast.

Noticing an anxious glance which the invalid cast toward the door, the old gentleman arose, and as he bent over her, asked:

"Was you thinking of the doctor, dear? He'll soon be along —he said he'd be here early!"

"No, it was not of him. He cannot save me!" replied the poor girl; "but I was thinking of my cousin. It is so strange that she has not come back. I do so want to see her before I die!"

"Don't talk of dying, dear," said the old man, brushing away a tear. "I don't see what can keep your cousin away!"

"I am afraid she has come to harm, sir," murmured the sick girl. "Though she has been very wicked—I know she is sorry for it—and her very tears proves that she loves me!"

"Yes, yes. But what harm could come to her?"

"I cannot tell, yet I feel as if it is so. I do so want to see her, and my uncle before I die!"

"You shall, if they can be found—I'll send Francis out to look after them—he'll be up here directly—ah, there's the doctor—I know his ring at the bell—it's quick and sharp, for he's always in a hurry!"

In a moment the doctor entered, and, hastening to the invalid's side, felt her pulse, and spoke kindly to her.

"I shall die, doctor!" she murmured. "You need not be afraid to tell me—I do not fear to die. I have prayed God to take me away, for I have had but little joy in life!"

The doctor was a stern man, he had been at many a death-bed; without a tremor he could even then have amputated an arm or a leg, but his lips quivered, and his eyes filled, as he gazed upon the young and patient sufferer.

"I will come again, by and bye!" he said, softly, and then he went out of the room. Mr Precise followed him.

33

" Will she live, doctor ?" he asked, when the door was closed behind him.

Tears gushed out of the doctor's eyes. "I was called too late !" he said. "The fever has gone, but it has carried her life with it—I could hardly feel her pulse, and her hand is cold as marble !"

"My God, how hard !" said the old man. "I've just learned to love her so, and I was agoing to adopt her—oh, it is too hard !" and the noble hearted old gentleman wept like a child.

"I will come again—but it is of no use ; she will not live till to-morrow morning !" said the doctor.

Mr. Precise tried to dry his eyes, and went into the room again, but Angelina saw plainly the traces of his tears.

"Do not weep for me, my dear, good friend !" she murmured. "It is best for me to go away. I have prayed God to take me home to him, and I hope he will. I have tried to be good, and often, often have I knelt down and prayed to Him to prepare me for death !"

"You're a living angel !" sobbed Mr. Precise—"I wish I could die in your place. I am an old body, and not worth much —but you're so good-hearted, you ought to live !"

The door opened, and Frank entered.

"You wanted me, Sir ?" said he, in a low tone.

"Yes, Francis. I wish you to go and hunt up the woman that was here yesterday morning. Big Lize, she is called, I believe !"

"But where can I find her ?" he asked.

"Somewhere in Thomas street, close to Church ; her poor cousin says. Now go and hunt everywhere—I want to see her very much ; she commenced telling me something yesterday !"

"What was it, sir ?" asked Frank, quickly.

"I don't exactly know, Francis, but tell her to come here quickly—I wish to see her—besides her poor cousin (Mr. P. said this in a whisper) is on her death-bed !"

"Poor creature !" said Frank, taking out his white handkerchief, and raising it to his eyes.

"You're a good boy, Francis—but now hurry away, and try and find her cousin !"

"Yes, sir," said Frank, but as soon as he got outside the door, he added, "*in a horn.*"

The meaning of that very popular phrase may not be understood by all our readers, but Frank meant by it, that he should not trouble himself much in the search for Lize.

"Things are coming to a head!" he muttered, as he stood upon the landing at the head of the stair-case. "Jack's men 'll be here to-night. I think I better mizzle now. With me, to go or not go, is the question. Whether it would be better to stay and see the fun out, or to make myself scarce. If I stay I'll have a scene—but there's precious little romance in a night-row, as Byron said of sea-sickness! Jenny is getting too loving also; her affection is rising very fast, and I reckon I'd better slope, for fear of accidents! But then——"

"Francis!" said his master, opening the door. "Ah, I'm glad you haven't gone yet. My new watch has run down, and I've lost the key or mislaid it!"

"Will mine fit it, sir?" asked the young villain.

It was tried, but would not do.

"Take my watch with you, then, Francis, and get a key that'll fit it—a common brass key 'll do just as well as any!"

The young villain's eyes glistened as he took the valuable watch, which had been bought to supply the place of that borrowed by Captain Tobin.

"Now, go on—but do you want anything more?" asked Mr. Precise, observing a hesitating look in Frank's face.

"Why, sir, if it wouldn't be too much trouble, I'd like to get fifteen dollars—it's my mother's rent day, and she hasn't enough to pay it!"

"You're a good boy—always dutiful, Francis!" replied the old gentleman, taking out his wallet, and unrolling some bills.

"Why, I havn't anything less than a fifty!" said he. "Never mind, Francis, get it changed, and bring me back the change, and do be quick!"

"Of course, sir," said Frank, pocketing the watch and money, and descending the stair-way.

"These are on my own hook!" he muttered, "and they're

sufficient reasons to decide me.   The die is cast—farewell to Jenny, and my secretaryship !"

Without taking a formal leave of the house-maid, Frank put on his over-coat and departed, putting his beautiful pocket edition of Shakspeare in his pocket, as also sundry other light but valuable articles, which he had collected in anticipation of this hour.   Among these was a stocking foot, which contained all of Jenny's earnings, for though Frank had objected to this appropriation when spoken of before the gang, he saw no reason for not taking it upon " his own hook."

CHAPTER III.

Big Lize was not a woman to despair—not one who would sink down and give way to weakness and tears, and when she found herself entrapped and caged by Circle, after a few shrieks and curses uttered in the bitterness of the moment, she rose from the damp ground where she had fallen, and began groping around to find what kind of a place she was in. It was utter darkness, but she soon found the wall, and by slowly traversing its sides, found that she was in a cell of about ten or twelve feet square, which was separated by a wall of stone from the outer cellar, next to the street, where old Jack kept his ales and liquors.

She of course did not know the thickness of this wall, but as she heard the noise of wagons and carts that were passing in the street, through it, a hope came to her heart that she might dig her way out. But she had no tools. She felt of the stones —they were small and irregular, of the kind generally used in building cellar walls, and cemented together with ordinary plaster.

At first she tried to tear out some of the stones; but in the effort she only lacerated her hands, without starting a single piece. Yet she had a weapon—what woman is there below the grade of the " upper-ten" who does not carry it ? She had *scissors* in her pocket.

She quickly tried them, and to her joy found that with their points she could scrape away the cement little by little. Yet it was a slow and a weary task, and after she had worked for hours, she had only got a little ways into the wall.

She knew the day had passed away, for she could hear the noise of the gang when they assembled in the evening, and as she paused from her labor to listen, she heard a plan laid out for robbing the house of Mr. Precise. The gang had received accurate information from Frank Hennock, and knew where everything lay, and even had prepared a key from an impression which Frank had taken, to open the little iron safe in which the old gentlemen kept his ready money.

And all of this time Lize was in agony. Her heart yearned to know where and how her wretched father was; her tortured fancy painted her poor cousin dying; and then her noble benefactor was to be robbed and ruined, and she who might have saved him was there a walled-in, helpless prisoner. She cursed, and raved, and tore her hair, but it was useless. A mocking laugh from the upper room was her only answer. She shouted for water, for her feverish lips were burning like fire, but not a drop could she get; she had eaten scarcely anything for two days, so exciting had been the scenes through which she had passed, yet not a mouthful of food was offered to her.

And yet she would not despair. With bleeding hands she worked on; now and then, it is true, she uttered a low moan, as her swollen heart would heave beneath the weight of its misery, but not a tear fell from her eyes. On through the long and weary watches of the night she toiled—after everything was still above her—careful to make no noise, yet scraping away in dust the cement which bound the stones of the wall together, and yet when the noise above and outside began again, and she knew thereby that another day had dawned, she had not cleared away more than six or eight inches in depth. True, she had loosened the way and taken out several of the stones, yet she began to grow weak, and her heart trembled when she thought that her strength would fail her before she could open a passage. Her only hope was in getting out in time to warn Mr. Precise, and she knew that it must be done by night, or at least, early in the evening.

Her thirst increased every moment, for her fever of course added to it, and time after time she raised her raw and bleeding fingers to her lips to suck them.

Some hours after daylight, however, she heard the trap door above her move, and quickly ceasing her work she cast herself upon the ground.

"'Ow're you are gittin' halong, 'old g'hal?" cried Circle.

"For God's sake give me some water!" moaned Lize in a piteous tone, not caring that the wretch should know how she was getting along.

"Summat vet, eh ? Vouldn't you like suthin' a leetle stronger than water ?" said he, in a bantering tone.

"Anything you like, Jack. Oh, do have mercy on me, I am dying !" moaned Lize in a still weaker tone, used purposely to deceive him. "Don't treat me worse than you would a dog! Indeed I'm dying !"

"That be blow'd !" cried Jack, roughly, " dyin' ar'n't so bloody heasy 's all that ! But I'll give you summat vet, for I don't mean to starve you to death. Vot 'll you 'ave—a pot o' 'alf-an-'alf, or a taste o' gin ?"

"Water, water, I'm in a burning fever !" moaned Lize.

"Well, then I'll give you some o' the jug diet—you're used to that !" said the old man, and closing the trap he went away.

He returned in a few minutes and opening it again, lowered down a basket which contained a jug of water and a loaf of bread.

"Thank God !" murmured Lize, as she saw this timely supply.

"Better thank me, hold g'hal !" cried Jack. "Take 'em out o' the basket, I want to 'aul it hup agin' !"

Lize took the water and bread—and Jack hauled up the basket and closed the trap over her.

She raised the jug to her lips and took a long, long draught of the cooling water.

"Thank God !" she murmured again, fervently

Oh, how sweet was that draught to her. Never tasted wine richer to an epicure—it was nectar to her.

And then she broke the loaf and ate ravenously. Not a gourmand in our city ever enjoyed a meal as she did that. She felt that it would give her strength to renew her work. She would have given anything to have bathed her hot brow and burning hands in the water, but she dared not—it was too precious.

After using a part of her food and water, she carried it near the place where she had been at work, and placing it carefully upon the ground renewed her labor. Her strength was much restored now, for hope again found a home in her heart. Though her hands were cut to the very bone with the sharp and jagged stones, she dug away during all of that live-long day. As she kept on, the sounds from the street came more plainly to her ears, and at last she actually got a glimpse of light, through a narrow crevice, where she had plucked away a small stone. And this was just at twilight, as she could see by the grey dimness which poured into the outer cellar through the glass window which lighted it. She took a hasty glance while it was yet light, to see how she could manage, when she got into the next room, to get into the street, and, while she was looking, got a glimpse of a pair of stout legs descending a ladder on the left, and as they were surmounted or rather surrounded by a set of exceedingly dirty petticoats, she rightly conjectured that they belonged to the old man's daughter "'Arriet." The said feminine came down to fill a decanter from one of the casks in the cellar, and as Lize listened carefully to the manner in which she returned and the sound made by the closing door at the head of the ladder, she was satisfied that it was only an ordinary trap-door, shutting down from above without locking.

The small window, level with the street which fronted the cellar, seemed to be the only other outlet, but Lize was not daunted by the difficulties which lay before her. She felt as if all would be over when once she had made her passage through the wall, and with renewed energy she worked on, only pausing now and then to wet her feverish lips with a sip of water.

Darkness closed in, and though she could no longer see the light in the next apartment, she could feel that every exertion served to increase the size of the aperture. She knew that she had but little time to spare, and though the pain of her wounded hands was intense, she kept on till the sound of the trap-door moving above her warned her to be on her guard.

"Ello, hold g'hal!" cried Jack Circle, from above, "ow're you gittin' on jist habout now?"

"When 're you going to let me out?" asked Lize, by way of a response to his question.

"Jist when we're ready, and not afore!" said Jack.

"Oh, don't hurry yourself!" said Lize, carelessly, "I'm very comfortable now since you gave me something to eat!"

"S'pose you are—you wouldn't like summat vet, eh?"

"I shouldn't wish to give you so much, trouble!" replied Lize.

"The trouble hisn't so much, Lize—you seem to take things, so heasy now, I don't mind sendin' you down a little suthin'; if you'll honly come hinter reason, I'll let you hout o' that in the mornin', maybe we'll want the place to stow haway swag in!"

"Thank ye, for nothing!" muttered Lize, but the old man didn't hear her. He had gone to bring her "summat vet."

"'Ere it is, hold g'hal!" said he, a moment after lowering down a small bottle of brandy. "I'll fling ye down a blanket bye 'n' bye—you must a 'ad a 'ard berth on't last night!"

"Shouldn't wonder if I had!" replied Lize, taking the bottle from the string, at once uncorking it and taking a sip of its contents.

Jack made no reply, but shut down the trap again, leaving her, as we must for the present, in the company of the brandy bottle.

Very questionable company, we hear a Crotonian reader say—questionable it may be, *spirited* it certainly is, and if of the quality usually vended at the fashionable " *dispensaries* " in Gotham, we have no hesitation in pronouncing it *evil*, or bad, confoundedly *bad*, if you like the word better. Liquor-dealers and milkmen must think themselves privileged characters in our city; they certainly are a sinful class, for they seem to make it a point never to deal in anything *pure*.

CHAPTER IV.

CHARLES MEADOWS was in the same upper room where Carl ton had held his former interviews with him. It was afternoon Wine and food were on the table. Though he had drank freely of the former, his face was ashy pale, and his whole appearance indicated that of a person struck with a deathly sickness.

Sam. Selden was seated near him, but he looked as composed and comfortable as ever, and very deliberately sipped his wine, now and then raising the glass between his eye and the window to admire its rich color.

"This *is* great wine!" said the gambler. "Carlton never gets it out except upon extraordinary occasions. He bought it of Osborn—a half-pipe imported on trial. It was too expensive for the general run of customers, but Carlton took a fancy to it, and where he takes a fancy, money is uncounted!"

"What time is it?" asked the clerk, gloomily, not heeding Sam.'s panegyric upon the wine.

"Seven minutes after four, precisely!" replied Selden, glancing at his watch.

"What time will it be dark?" continued the clerk, without raising his eyes, which were gloomily fixed on the table.

"About seven, that is twilight, it'll not be really *dark* before half-past!"

"Only three hours!" muttered the clerk, with a sigh. "Only three hours. My God, how time flies to-day!"

"It's been rather heavy on my hands," said Sam., carelessly ; "I've not even taken my customary stroll along Broadway, to see the fashions. I wonder if I haven't been missed by some of the dem'd fascinating promenaders, who're there as regular as the sunshines, to see and be seen!"

The cogitations of Selden were cut short by the entrance of Carlton, who cried :

" Well, Boys, how're you passing the time—find that wine rich, eh ?"

" The wine is demnition good !" replied Selden ; " but our friend Charley seems to be in the dumps—it don't wake him up !"

" Come, come, Meadows, cheer up. Take another glass— there's no use in being dumpy !. Everything is fixed now !" said Carlton.

At the same time, he put a small pistol case down upon the table, and, taking a pistol from it, added :

" See there ! I've just been cleaning that little beauty, and loading it up. I'll bet it'll go off as clear as a rocket !"

Meadows looked at the weapon, and shuddered, but did not speak.

" What's the matter, Charley, you're not going to flunk out, are you ?" asked Carlton, noticing the shudder.

" *No*, sir !" said the clerk, in a tone so quick, deep and harsh, that Carlton involuntarily started, " *No*, sir ; I shall do *my* part, be ready to do *yours !*"

" Certainly, my dear fellow, but you needn't scare a man to death. Come, take a glass of wine, and compose yourself !"

" I will drink no more !" replied the clerk, gloomily, taking up the pistol, and handling it in a manner so careless, that it alarmed Carlton, toward whom it was accidentally pointed.

" Look out there, Charley—be careful how you handle that weapon !" he cried ; " it's loaded to go off !"

" So I suppose ; but you needn't fear, it'll not go off before the time—seven, half-past seven, it'll be dark, then !" replied the clerk, in the same calm and gloomy tone.

" Yes, that'll be about the time—did you go over the ground and see how it lay ?"

" Yes !" replied the clerk.

" Don't you think my plan is well laid ?" continued Carlton.

" Yes !" said Meadows, without raising his eyes from the weapon which he held.

" If you follow it in every particular there will not be the slightest danger.   After you are clear, go home quietly, and go to sleep !"

"Sleep ? ha ! ha !" wildly laughed the clerk.   "I expect to sleep *very* sound—don't *you ?*"

"Just as usual.   You make a great deal more of this matter than I would !" replied the gambler.

"Oh, no, I consider it a trifling thing.   It is *only* a *murder !*" replied the clerk, in a bitterly sarcastic tone.

"Have you tried on the dress, yet ?" asked Carlton, wishing to alter the tone of the conversation.

"Yes !"

"Does it fit ?   Can you move easily in it ?"

"Well enough !" responded the clerk, moodily.

"Well, then, all is fixed—there will be nothing to prevent its success.   But you must go home at once, after the work is done —and then go to your store in the morning as usual !   This will be necessary, to avoid exciting suspicion.   You'll have to keep your ears open, and your lips shut too, after it is all over. I shall have some trouble—but nothing can be *proved* against me, the whole affair 'll blow over in a week or two !"

The clerk made no reply, but sat with his head bent down, gazing upon the pistol as he had before.

"This is dull, really ; Sam., join me in a glass of wine !" said Carlton, who in spite of his assumed indifference and calmness, felt more and more nervous, as the hour of his purposed revenge approached.

When the two had filled their glasses, Carlton again spoke to Meadows.

"You'd better take another glass of wine, Charley !" said he.

"Give me some brandy—let it be strong as *fire !*" said the clerk, sternly.

"Why, you don't mean to get drunk?   That would never do !"

"*Drunk !*" repeated the young man in a bitter tone.   "You've not liquor enough in your house to make me drunk *now !*   I am weak, I want brandy to strengthen me !"

Carlton went to a cupboard, in a corner of the room, took a sealed bottle out of it, and, after brushing away the dust, drew the cork.

" There," said he, as he put it before Meadows, " is some that's older than either of us ! It was bottled in 1801—I got it of Rachau in '40 !"

Meadows made no reply, except by pouring out a tumbler half full of it, and drinking it down raw.

In a few minutes it seemed to have produced an effect—his cheeks lately so pale, flushed up—his eyes sparkled, and rising from his chair, he paced to and fro across the floor with a firm, quick step.

Carlton looked at him anxiously—he feared that the liquor had been too strong, and would disable the clerk from his purposed deed. Meadows saw the look—divined its meaning. Smiling, he said :

"You need not fear me now—it was just what I wanted—I *was* weak in heart and body—but I'm all right now !"

"I'm glad of it !" replied Carlton. " The hour is near—but you must remember all the directions."

"You need not fear for me now. Though flushed, I am calm and strong !" replied Meadows.

"Suppose you put on the dress, and let me see how you look !" said Carlton.

"Certainly !" replied the clerk, proceeding to put a woman's frock on over his other clothes. Taking off his cap, he put that in his pocket, and then put on a common bonnet, which was covered with a green veil. The dress which was perfectly loose at the waist, so as to be easily taken off, was covered by a large shawl, and the disguise was finished.

"How do I look ?" asked the clerk, as he stepped mincingly across the room, endeavoring to imitate the inimitable walk of woman.

"Capital! Very like a lady—but not much like my wife !' said Carlton. " But you'll do ! You saw the place where you was to throw in the dress ?"

" Yes !"

"Have you the lead attached to it ?"

"Yes ; and to the shawl and bonnet ! I'll see that they're put out of sight—they'll never *rise* against me !"

"Well, then, all will be right—but be careful that you're not observed on the dock!"

"Oh, never fear! It'll be quite dark when I get down there!" replied Meadows.

"So it will—and here it is, after *five* already! I must go and see my wife. Sam. 'll keep you company till I come back!" said Carlton, and passing through into his wife's apartments, he left them together, as we must also do, for the present.

CHAPTER V.

"I BELIEVE we'll soon have that villain Genlis in our power, Annie!" said Mr. Abingdon, as he entered his wife's sitting-room, a short time after the date of our last scene there.

"How, dear Edward? tell me!" quickly responded the anxious wife.

"Why, when I went to our good friend M—— and told him all of the circumstances, he at once started out with me to visit the various Hack stands, to see if we could not find the driver who had taken you to the house of Genlis.

"We went to the stand at the Park—to that in Chatham Square, and to several of the largest stables, but found no team corresponding to the one you described, nor any coach with the tassel mutilated. We had almost given up the hunt in despair, when M—— remarked that sometimes a coach or two was to be found at the junction of Hudson street and West Broadway. We hurried down there, and sure enough a coach was there, with a team answering your description.

"The moment M—— glanced at it, and saw the driver, he said, 'that we were on the right clue.' The owner of the hack, it appeared, was a fellow very appropriately called 'Dirty-faced Jack,' but he was not with the hack at the time, one of his hands, Mr. Terrence O'Grady, being in charge of the vehicle.

"Terrence knew the magistrate in a moment, and when he saw us stop and examine his coach, he started off at a run, intending to make himself 'scarce' as they say in the West. But M—— gave chase and overhauled him in a moment.

"'Where were you going to, you scoundrel?' he cried. 'What do you mean by running away from an officer of the law.'

"'Och! yer honer is intirely mistaken! I was only goin' afther my dinner!' replied Terrence.

"'Your dinner, at this time of day, you scoundrel? Why it's five o'clock!' said M——.

"'But, yer honer, Biddy has got to be very fashionable, o' late times! We always git our praties an' beef at five!' responded Terrence.

"'Ah, very well. We'll take a look in your carriage!' said M—— opening the hack door, and looking at the tassels hanging by the side.

"They were the same color of the cord we had, and we at once detected the place where you had cut it off. So, you see, Annie, that little thoughtless act has turned out to be greatly serviceable!"

"Thank Heaven!" replied the young wife—"but go on, Edward, and tell me the rest!"

"When we found by the tassel that we had the right coach, M—— turned to Terrence, and said in a stern, harsh tone:

"'You've been carrying on a nice business, haven't you?'

"'I've never done anythin' that my masther didn't bid me to!' replied the fellow.

"'Then he told you to do all this work for Genlis, eh?'

"At the name of Genlis, the fellow's confidence forsook him entirely.

"'Och, botheration take 'em all! I tould 'em it 'ud come to this!' he cried, and then turning to M——, he added:

"'For the love o' heaven an' all the saints, Mr. M——, do let me off this wonst! I'll quit drivin', and nivir another box 'll I sit on, till I go to my own funeral!'

"'There's only one way to get out of the scrape, and you may choose between that and cutting stones in Sing-Sing!' replied M——, sternly.

"'Then spake it out, yer honer—an' it's myself, Terrence O'Grady, that'll do yer biddin' ony day, rather than look inside o' the grey walls. Faith, the outside on 'em looks worse 'an the small-pox!' said Terrence, pale with fear.

"'You've got to tell me where this Genlis lives, and at the same time say nothing to put him or your dirty-faced master on their guard!'

"'Faith, yer honer, that's all as asy as prayin'; the ould

Gipsey don't live a dozen blocks from yer honer's office. It's round in W—— street !'

" ' Don't tell a falsehood ! Why did you drive so far, if the place is so near !'

" ' 'Caze, it was orders. I druv around up one street and down another, so's to make the visitors belave he lives in the counthry. He has a man that meets 'em where I lave's 'em, and walks 'em round his garden an' all that, so the craters git turned round an' round, till they forgit everythin' !'

"But to make the story short, Annie, M—— and myself found out all we wanted from the hackman, and he is bribed and frightened completely into our service. To-night M—— will surround it with a party of policemen. You will soon hear from your boy, I hope, for M—— and I will force the secret out of this villain, and see what his magic is made of !"

"But he might, in revenge, destroy our child, if he is yet living !"

"No ; hemp is too cheap here for him to dare that. Our plan is well laid and it cannot fail. But you will have to take a share in it !"

"What part, my husband ?" asked the wife.

"You will go to Julia, as you have done before, and tell her that you must see Genlis again. Offer the usual fee—and the carriage will doubtless be sent as before. M—— and myself wish to catch this Genlis in his mummery, it may be of use in recovering our Willie !"

"But will you be near me ? I should be afraid of that Genlis, if I were alone with him, and he knew that I had told of him !"

"You need not fear—I shall be near. Now go to Julia the Indian woman, and tell her you must see Genlis again—that you will pay his usual fee. We'll make him disgorge the money soon enough !"

"I will do as you wish, dear husband. Oh, I pray God that we may get back our boy !"

"We will, Annie, we will—be hopeful. I feel confident now that we are on the right track !"

3

CHAPTER VI

The grey of twilight had deepened the shadows and drawn its misty veil over the city. The streets were crowded by poor sewing, and binding girls, who, having worked as long as they could see, were now hurrying homeward, wearied in body and spirit, for where labor is illy paid for, the spirit may not be glad.

At this hour, Charles Meadows, closely veiled and disguised as a woman, passed out from the dwelling of Henry Carlton, and walked slowly along through back streets toward the central part of the town.

In a few moments after, Mrs. Carlton left the same house, and, with a hurried, tremulous step, passed on up Broadway.

Her time and pace was so well suited with that of Meadows, that when she passed the corner of the street which intersected Broadway, near the place of Cooly, she saw the tall figure of the disguised clerk cross the street before her, and take his appointed position in the shaded niche of a closed-up door way, a short distance down the cross street, to the right.

Her duty had already been given to her. She passed on to the saloon of the fated Cooly, and it seemed that he expected her, for he stood at the door, whistling a careless air.

She beckoned him out to her, and he advanced to her side.

"Good evening, Hannah," said he, in his usual tone. "Are you well to-night? You seem to be all in a tremble!"

"I have cause to tremble, Charles. I am sick at heart and wretched. Will you walk a little way with me? I would talk to you!"

"Yes; but I can't spare many minutes. I expect some friends every moment, whom I promised to meet!"

"You need not spare *many* minutes—it'll not take long!" said the woman, in a deep, unnatural tone. "I have only a few questions to ask, and you can answer them as we walk on. We'll just step around the corner of the next street. It is dark there now, and we can talk unobserved!"

"That's true, my dear; but what questions did you speak of?"

"The most important is this. Why have you deserted me, after blasting my name and rendering me an unhappy, wretched creature?"

"Why, the fact is, Hannah, you know as well as I do, that we were doing wrong, and I thought the best way was to drop our intimacy!"

"Why did you not think of the *wrong*, before you drew me away from my husband's side?" exclaimed the woman, bitterly.

"Why, my dear, to tell the truth, I didn't think it was wrong just then, myself!"

"No, not until you was tired of my society—satiated with my poor beauty. Like the ungrateful bee, you deserted the flower as soon as it had lost the honey of novelty. And now I suppose you'll seek some other helpless female, and damn another soul into eternal misery and infamy!"

"Poh, Hannah, you are running romance into the ground!"

"There is more reality in this business than romance, sir!" said the woman, sternly.

"Very well, my dear, have it your own way; but if you have anything more to say, be quick—I've no time to spare!"

"Very little, I acknowledge," said Mrs. Carlton, stopping on the side walk, in the dense shadow of the tall house before them. In the deeper shadow of the old door-way, she could see a dark object standing motionless. It was not five steps from where she was standing. Not a breath could be heard from him, yet it was Charles Meadows, upon his post.

Mrs. C. had so arranged Cooly that his back was directly toward this spot, and she now paused to say a few words to the victim, ere she gave the signal for his death.

"I have but little to say, Charles," she continued, "and what I have to say, is the last I have to utter to you in this world!"

"Then it'll be short and sweet!" said he, laughingly.

"Charles!" replied she, in a solemn tone, "this is no time for you to *jest*!"

"Well, well! Go on, and say what you have to say quick !" said he, rather impatiently.

"Then hear me. You won my love at a time when I fancied myself neglected by my husband. I gave you a fond and disinterested love—would have died to save you from pain and trouble !"

She paused a moment, but Cooly made no response, and she went on.

"When we separated the last time—I told you if you cast my love from you to beware of my *hate !*"

"So you did; but you needn't talk of hating me, Hannah, after the happy hours we've spent together !"

"Hush, sir, hush !" cried the woman, huskily. "Dare not to speak of them. I now *hate* you—stop, you must not move yet. It is not quite time—I've a few more words to say !"

Unwillingly, Cooly paused and listened, and at the same moment the dark shadow in the back ground, slowly and cautiously moved from its position.

The woman went on.

"Yes, Charles Cooly, I have fondly, deeply, madly *loved* you, and now, all as madly do I hate you. I have come here to take my last farewell of you !"

"Well, Hannah, I'm agreed—let's kiss, however, and part friends !"

"Ha ! ha !" she cried, with a wild laugh, "Judas betrayed with a kiss, so will I !"

The shadow of the murderer was over them, as the victim bent down and met the woman's kiss ; then in the very second after, she sprung one step aside, and said :

"*It is time.* Good bye, Charles Cooly !"

At the same instant, a blinding flash of light illumined the darkness—a quick, sharp report was heard, and as she turned and fled with bird-like speed down the street, Charles Cooly tumbled forward upon the pavement, with a bullet in his brain. The murderer, Charles Meadows, dropped the pistol beside the corpse, and with hurried steps crossed Broadway, and dashed down the dark street beyond.

"Go it, girl ! Let your legs do their duty !" cried a couple of careless persons, passing up Broadway, who saw as they supposed, only some unhappy courtesan, who had got in a a scrape.

They might easily have stopped him—but he rushed on, leaving a terrible scene of excitement behind him, for in a moment the body of Cooly was discovered by persons rushing to the spot, attracted by the report of the pistol.

Meadows stopped at a little dark alley, a short distance down the street, and quickly divested himself of the female apparel, which he hurriedly tied up in a small bundle. He then passed rapidly down to the North River, and in ten minutes from the moment when he fired the pistol, the female dress was sunk in the muddy waters of the river.

One would think, that having done this much toward his security, and having been unfollowed, and passed unquestioned so far, he would be less agitated than at first. But it was not so. When he hurried along an unfrequented street, toward his mother's house, his limbs trembled beneath him—he was ghastly pale, sick at heart and in body. The peculiar excitement which had sustained him until the deed was done, had now failed him, and a very hell of terror and remorse was raging in his bosom.

As fast as he could, he rushed along till he reached his mother's door, and just as his foot touched the door step, the door opened, and a blaze of light, from the hall-lamp, almost blinded him.

"Here he is!" cried the voice of a man, in the entry, "here he is at last!"

Charles was so terrified, that he could not even fly, though he thought that the officers of the law were before him. With a bitter groan of agony, he sunk fainting upon the threshold.

"What is the matter, my son?" asked his mother, bending over him, anxiously, then turning to the person who had spoken first, she added:

"Do help me in with him. The poor boy is sick—he has a fit or something!"

"Yes, ma'am—you jist stand aside a bit, I'll lift him up, and tote him in! Why, what's the matter, Charley?" cried the young man.

"Who are you? Are you not an officer?" asked the clerk, raising up his head with a wild, quick glance.

" An ossifer? Well, that's rich! No; don't you know me, Charley? I'm *Mose*—your old school-mate, *Mose!*" and as he spoke, the young man lifted the clerk up, and helped him into the house.

" Did you hear of it so soon?" continued the clerk, looking stupidly at Mose.

" Hear of it? The poor creetur told me of it herself, this mornin', and I've been a lookin' for you all day, to go with me, and my crowd, to help her out o' the muss !"

" Her? What do you mean? It was a *man* that I——'

" A man !" interrupted Mose—" No, 'twas your own sister 'Bell! I seen her this mornin' out o' old Ma'am Swett's winder —see here, she drapt this into my cart !"

Meadows looked at the paper which Isabella had written that morning, and then while he grew more pale, if possible than before, he asked in a choked and husky voice :

" Did you say you saw her ?"

" Yes," replied Mose, "and I told her to hold on till night, that we'd be there—and now I'm ready to go *in*, Charley! Me and Sikesey—he's jist round the corner, with four or five more that runs with our machine. We've got a gallus machine now, Charley—it's been to the shop, and looks jist like new !"

" Do hurry off, and rescue your sister, from that dreadful place, Charles !" cried Mrs. Meadows. "My dream has come true !"

" Yes, both of them ! *both* of them, mother !" cried the clerk, wildly.

She gave one searching look at him—his very manner seemed to answer her, and she screamed :

" Oh, holy God of Heaven, if it is so, I shall go mad !"

She comprehended in a moment, why he had taken Mose for an officer.

" Leave us alone, for one minute !" she cried, to Mose—" leave us alone for one minute—I must talk to him !"

" Sartinly, ma'am !" said Mose,--" he'll find me and Sikesey at the corner, and I hope he'll not be long a comin' !"

" No, I'll be there in a minute !" said Meadows.

The next moment mother and son were alone.

" What is it, Charles, you have to tell me ! You said both my dreams had come true !"

" Yes, if my sister is ruined, they have !" said the young man, hoarsely. " It is not an half hour since I *killed* a man !"

" Killed ?" shrieked the mother. " Oh, my God, what will we come to ? Was it this Whitmore ?"

" No, no ! I wish it was ! His time is yet to come—my hand is in now, and there's no use for me to stop !"

" God have mercy on me ! I shall go mad !" groaned the mother.

" You must keep still, mother ! If you hear of a man being shot to-night, you mus'n't say a word. No one knows that *I* did it ! I didn't mean to tell you—but I couldn't help it !"

The mother was too much shocked to reply. She burst into tears. Charles could not endure her misery. Begging her, for his sake, to be calm and silent, he hurried out to seek Mose and his party, and with them, to search after his ill-fated sister.

One glance at Mrs. Carlton, before we close this chapter. When she heard the report of Meadows' pistol, she did not wait to see the wretched victim fall—she did not dare to turn one glance that way, but rushed down the street and turned the next corner, with all the speed which terror could give to her agile limbs. Breathless, and trembling in every joint, she reached the door of her husband's house.

He was there, awaiting her.

" Is it done ?" he asked.

" Yes, oh, God, yes !" she gasped, and would have fallen upon the threshold, had he not caught and steadied her.

" Be calm, Hannah, be calm. Everything depends on our mutual self-possession, now !" he said. " I know we will be suspected—the officers will doubtless soon be here—hurry up and change your dress, hide your shoes, there is mud on them ! I must go into the faro-room. It will not do for me to be absent a moment !"

With a strong effort, the wife recovered herself and hurried to her room, when she instantly locked herself in, while Carlton took his place at his faro-table again.

As he expected, in a few moments the police entered his room, and he was told that he was a prisoner.

"For what, gentlemen?" he asked, in apparent surprise, knowing of course, that *here*, in this most *moral* city (God forgive me for that lie), he never would be arrested for mere gambling.

The officers would not tell, but closely searched his person, and examined him from head to foot. He was unarmed. His boots were clean, the blacking unsoiled and bright. He evidently had not been out in the muddy streets.

"Have you been here all the evening?" asked the magistrate, who headed the party.

"Yes, sir. I believe I've not been out of the house since dinner!" said the gambler, calmly.

"What is the time?" asked the same officer.

"Eight, nearly; it wants eleven minutes, by the clock on St. Paul's; I noticed at seven, when the clock struck, that my watch was ten minutes too slow. I remarked it, didn't I Sam.?"

"Yes, sir, I believe you did!" replied Selden, to whom Carlton had spoken.

The magistrate eyed Selden very closely, but both these persons were so perfectly calm, that his sagacity was put completely at fault.

"Is your wife at home?" asked the magistrate.

"I presume so!" replied Carlton. "She would not be likely to go out on such an evening! I'll go and see, if you wish!"

"No, sir, stay here for the present, under charge of one of my officers. If you will call a servant, and permit me to be shown to her rooms, I'll be obliged to you!" said the magistrate.

"Certainly, sir, but this conduct is *very* singular," replied Carlton.

"It may be, but it is *necessary!*" replied the magistrate, sternly.

Carlton sent a black waiter after Eliza, Mrs. C.'s waiting woman.

"Eliza," said Carlton, when she made her appearance, "is your mistress in?"

"Yes, sir, I s'pect so. She was unwell all the afternoon, and has been locked in her room all the evening!" replied the mulatto woman.

"Show me to her room, instantly!" said the magistrate, sternly.

Then bidding two of his subordinates remain in charge of Carlton, and not permit him to hold communication with any one, the officer followed Eliza up stairs.

The door of Mrs. Carlton's room was locked, but after some difficulty it was opened, and Mrs. C. appeared in a loose undress, with no signs about her, of having been in the street. She was pale, and very much agitated, and when asked what was the matter, only replied, that she was sick, and had been so all day. She acted her part far less calmly than her husband had done—but still she succeeded so far, as to put the officers of the law completely at fault.

They had already learned, that a woman had been seen with Cooly, but a moment before his body was found—they had learned, that immediately after the report of the pistol was heard, a woman was seen to cross Broadway very hurriedly, and as it was publicly known that she had been intimate with Cooly, and that her husband's jealousy and anger had been aroused, suspicion at once pointed her out as an accomplice in the murder, if not indeed the murderer. But there was no sign to sustain the suspicion—no proof to fix the crime upon her, or her husband.

CHAPTER VII.

It was an unfortunate thing for poor Isabella, that Mose turned his cart around, and went back to ask her if she was not "'Bell Meadows." He was seen, and overheard, by Madame S.

"So, ho!" muttered the woman, after he had passed, "the bird thinks she can get out of the cage. I'll have to clip her wings!"

The wretch instantly called her cook.

"Make a nice breakfast for the girl in the garret," said she. "Some strong coffee, mutton chops and the like, and bring it to me, I'll carry it up myself!"

The breakfast was soon prepared, and brought up to the landlady, who went to a private cupboard, and brought a phial, from which she poured a drug into the coffee.

Isabella was seated at the table reading the Bible, when Madame S. went in. She shuddered, as she looked at the hag, but did not move from her seat.

"I've brought you some breakfast, my girl!" said the landlady, more kindly than she had spoken before. "I'm sorry I was so harsh just now, but I've such a set here, they'd put a saint out of patience sometimes! Do eat a little, I know you must be hungry!"

"Thank you, I cannot eat!" replied Isabella, tearfully, "but if you'll give me a glass of water, I'll thank you!"

"Wont coffee do as well—there's some that's nice and strong!" said the woman.

"I could not swallow it—I only want a little water!" said the young girl, who did not suspect that the coffee was drugged.

"Well, I'll get you some!" said the old woman, and she again left the room, locking, it as usual, behind her.

She again went to her cupboard, for she was prepared even for this wish of Isabella's. She took a paper which contained a small white powder, and putting about a teaspoonful into a glass nearly full of water, added a little sugar, and then cut a lemon, and squeezed some of the juice into it.

"That'll take away the taste!" she muttered, and hurried again to the garret.

"I made some nice lemonade—it's so cooling, and allaying to thirst!" said she, as she entered.

Isabella's lips were parched with fever, and she drank it off in a moment, without a thought of its contents.

"I'll leave the breakfast—you may want it by and bye!" said the woman, with a smile; and then she left Isabella alone.

"It will soon be night," murmured the wretched girl, "and then I hope and pray God, that I shall be rescued from here."

She continued to read on—but she became sleepy in a little while, and still without a thought of the cause of her sudden drowsiness, she laid down upon the bed, and went into a sound sleep.

In a few moments Madame S. returned, and smiled as she saw how well her potion had operated.

Calling a servant, she and the negress lifted the poor girl from the couch, and carried her down into a small cell in the back part of the cellar of the house, which was sunk into the ground beyond the regular cellar wall, and closed by a secret door, which never would be observed by a careless searcher.

"The devil couldn't find her, now!" said the landlady, with a satisfied tone; "her friends may come as soon as they like!"

Isabella was indeed in a dangerous situation now. She was beyond the aid which she had solicited, and which had been promised her—she was entirely in the power of one who would sell her own *soul* for gold, and who cared less for the virtue of her sex, except as a matter of trade, than she did for the clouds that swept across the sky.

We will at once pass over the time intervening between that hour and night, and introduce a new scene to our readers.

Maddened by his own remorse, as well as the thought that his sister was in a den of prostitution, and had probably been ruined, Charles Meadows, with Mose and his party, reached the door of the house where she was confined.

The first intimation Madame S. got of their arrival, was by the ringing of the bell, and the voice of Mose. She hurried to the door, and asked in her usual tone, what was wanted.

"We're jist payin' you a friendly wisit, Ma'am, that's all; let's in, will ye?" said Mose.

"Certainly," replied the "she boss" opening the door, readily; "what can I do for you, gentlemen?"

"You can jist show us the way up to your upper story with a candle, and be hasty about it, you thievin' old catamaran!" replied Mose, planting himself firmly in the hall.

"I'd like to know what you want to do in my fourth story, or garret?" said Ma'am S.

"We only want a g'hal that you've got stowed away there, you everlastin' lump o' sin!"

"There's no one there?" said the woman, quietly.

"What! D'you go for to say that 'Bell Meadows, Charley Meadows' sister, he that's here alongside o' me, aint up there?"

"There was a Miss Meadows slept there with her beau last night, but she's gone away with him to day!" replied the harridan.

"Lookee, old woman, that's gass!" cried Mose. "We've come here after that same little g'hal, and you've got to show her up, or we'll down with your rascally old crib, that's all!"

"You may look the house over, from top to bottom!" replied the landlady, indignantly. "As I said before, there was a Miss Meadows slept here last night with her beau, but they both went away, about dinner time!"

"Gass! Let's search the house!" cried Mose, and in a moment, all of his party, except two, whom he told to look out for the door, were scattered about the house, searching every apartment. The garret was found empty, and of course the search was in vain, though they looked from the roof to the cellar.

Charles Meadows was fearfully excited. He knew that his sister had been there—the note which Mose had received, told how unwillingly—and now he knew not where to look for her. His imagination painted her agonizing misery—his heart was full of remorse and wretchedness—it was a burning hell within a hell.

"What was the name of the man that brought her here?" he asked, as after the vain search, he confronted the wretch who kept the house.

"He didn't give any name—he was a foreigner!" replied the woman, boldly.

"Are you sure it was not Whitmore, or Livingston? Speak, you hag, or I'll murder you!"

"No; he was not an American, he was a Spaniard, I think!" replied the woman, undaunted by his wild and haggard looks, and threatening tone.

"Where did they go to?—Did she go unwillingly?" continued the wretched brother.

"I don't know where they went. She went away willing enough, more willing than she came?"

"God of Heaven, she is ruined!" moaned the brother.

"Then the old crib, shall pay for it!" shouted Mose, and as he spoke, he raised a mahogany chair and dashed it into a large pier glass which fronted the parlor.

"Go in, boys—let the she boss suffer; but don't hurt the g'hals!" he continued. "Go in, Sikesey, don't be afeared!"

"Watch, murder! help!" shouted the landlady, as she saw her best furniture dashed into pieces. But no watch came; rows were too common in that neighborhood for them to notice, and in less than the time we take to tell the story, Ma'am S. saw every window in her rooms broken—her sofa-cushions cut up—chandaliers dashed into atoms, chairs crushed down in a heap in the middle of the floor.

"There's no use in stayin' here, Charley!" said Mose, when the furniture was nearly all demolished—"your poor sister aint here—but we'll look 'round the whole row of wimmen shops, till we find her!"

Meadows was nearly delirious. He was fit then for any deed. Murder would have been but pastime to him.

"Have you any idea who it was that took her there?" asked Mose, when he stood in the street once more.

"No, not without it was one Whitmore—but I heard he was

laid up with a broken arm and head—he got into a row in Broadway last night !"

"Maybe 'twas him that I lammed !" said Mose. "I gave some dandy chap thunder over the cocoa-nut, last night !"

"I must see him !" said Charley, "he *must* know how my sister came to leave his sister's house !"

"Sartin. Let's go and see what he's got to say about it !" cried Mose. "Come along, Sikesey—b'hoys, come alo-o-ong !"

CHAPTER VIII.

At last the hole in the cellar wall was large enough for Lize to creep through it. But it was very late before the work was accomplished. It seemed to Lize, that she had been hours, long weary hours in getting out the last stone—yet it was not quite midnight, when she passed through the aperture, and stood in the outer cellar. She paused here, and took the last sip of liquor which was left in her bottle, and rested a moment to collect her energies for a bold and desperate attempt to escape.

By the noise above her, she knew that there were plenty of old Jack's peculiar customers in the bar-room, and as she must pass through it, this added to her danger. But she felt confident that if she could once gain the street, she would be safe, for they would not dare to pursue her, and even if they did she was as speedy as she was nettlesome.

For a moment she paused to listen, and then ascended the stair-case or ladder, and put her broad shoulders against the trap-door. Something heavy was upon it—but she gave a sudden heave; it yielded, and the next moment she was up in the liquor shop. Without waiting an instan,t she leaped over the bar, and before any one could stir to intercept her, she was in the street, running with her utmost speed toward the house of Mr. Precise.

The people in the bar-room were struck perfectly dumb with surprise. This was a performance " not down in the bill," and they couldn't comprehend it.

" 'Arriet" had been standing upon the trap, when Lize hove it up, and in so doing capsized her entirely over the bar, leaving her upon the floor, head down, displaying to an admiring set of thieves and topers, a pair of red and dumpy limbs, which like her face, appeared to be decidedly opposed to the " water cure" system.

Old Jack was in the back room, but startled by the outcry and crash, he rushed into the bar-room only in time to pick up his daughter, and learn that a ghost in petticoats, or something else had pitched "'Arriet" over the counter, and then " sloped" through the front door.

He quickly stepped behind the bar, and seeing that the trap was open, took a light, and descending, soon discovered the state of affairs.

"Blast the bloody fool!" he cried, as he emerged from the cellar, "I vos agoin' to let 'er hout in the mornin'! But it vont make much hodds, I reckon—for Jack Murphy, Bill, and the rest of 'em 'ave cleaned hout the hold un's crib afore this!"

Then he took a huge and ancient looking silver watch from his pocket, and glancing around at his customers, said :

"It's arter twelve, my chums, jist a minit, and that's shuttin' hup time, you know. Take vot you want and be hoff!"

Some of the topers who were possessed of the "ready," took something more to drink, and made their exits ; others, who were less fortunate, quietly dropped off, after taking a last lingering glance at the bar and its charms

When Lize got into the street, she did not stop to learn what damage she had done, either to Miss "'Arriet" or to the establishment—she did not even pause to listen whether she was pursued or not, but hearing the sound of some distant church-clock striking twelve, she rushed wildly on toward the street where Mr. Precise dwelt. Once a watchman attempted to stop her, but she had no time to explain, and settled his anxiety with a blow between the eyes which left him in a pleasant state of unconsciousness, reposing in the gutter, until she was a long ways beyond his precinct.

It seemed as if she could not get along fast enough, though she ran with all her speed, but at last she reached the house of Mr. Precise.

She was about to rush up the steps and ring the bell, when she saw that a basement window was open, and she determined to enter quietly in that way, and if possible to alarm the house, and prevent the thieves, whom she supposed to be inside, from carrying off their plunder.

She quickly entered the window. All was dark and silent within, but having once passed in by the basement, she remem bered the course which would lead to the room of Mr. Precise, and silently, breathlessly, hurried on up the first stair-case. But at the head of it she unfortunately stumbled, and in trying to save herself from falling, caught at the baluster of the stairway, which gave way with a loud crash.

"Damnation—we're nabbed!" cried a hoarse voice, and at the same time a blaze of light from the opened lens of a dark lantern almost blinded her, and she saw by its light four men with black silk handkerchiefs drawn over their faces, who were coming from the back parlor, loaded with plunder.

She could not recognize them, but they knew her, for they all cried out,

"It's big Lize—she's blowed on us!"

Lize screamed loudly for help, and tearing out one of the rounds from the broken baluster, attempted to prevent them from escaping, but the foremost villian, with a bitter curse, rushed upon her, and broke down her guard with a short iron crowbar, or "billy," as the burglars term it, and struck her another terrible blow over the shoulder.

But the heroic girl grappled with him in an instant, and screamed still louder for help. Lights were now seen flashing from above—the house was alarmed, and the villian whom she had grappled with, drew a short, heavy bowie knife, and drove it home to the very hilt in her breast, shouting to the rest,

"It's no time for play, grab all you can and run for it!"

Lize felt the keen weapon as it dashed into her very vitals, and with a piercing scream let go her hold, and fell to the bottom of the stairs. The burglars rushed out, trampling upon her as they passed over her form, and in a few moments had fled far away from the spot. Meantime Mr. Precise and Jenny hurried down the stairs, the former carrying a large pistol, which he always kept in his bed-room, though it had never been loaded since he possessed it, and Jenny, armed with the poker, both screaming watch, and robbers!

By the time they had got to poor Lize, a violent ringing was heard at the front door, which proved to be by the watchman,

35

who, as is customary in such cases, had arrived a moment too late to do any good. Letting him in, Mr. Precise hurried to the side of poor Lize, and raised her partly up.

"I'm done for," she muttered, "but I tried my best to save you!"

"What is it? why you're dreadfully wounded! what is the matter!" cried Mr. Precise, nervously, not being able to comprehend the nature of things at all, but seeing that she was bleeding terribly.

"Run for a doctor," he added, to the watchman—"run as hard as you can!"

"But haven't you been robbed? Isn't she one of the robbers?" urged the official, who "of course" thought if she was a criminal, that the getting a surgeon would be unnecessary trouble.

"Never mind what she is, go for a doctor—I don't care if I have been robbed, run for a doctor!" cried Mr. Precise, very impatiently.

"You'd better go yourself, sir!" said the watchman, "I'll stay here to guard the prisoner!"

"To guard one that's dying! You're a rum copper, you are!" said Lize, faintly, casting a look of scorn upon the officer. Then looking at Mr. Precise, she said:

"You needn't send for any doctor for me. It's all over. When the knife's pulled out, I shall go off! Do take me up to Angelina, if she's alive yet!"

"Oh, yes, and she's very bad off—but I'd a'most forgotten her in this new trouble!" cried Mr. Precise. "Oh, dear me, what a terrible time I do have. One poor angel of a creetur dyin' up stairs, and another down here! What shall I do! Jenny run for a doctor!"

"And call two or three of my mates here; holler like mad when you git to the corner, and when they come arter you, send 'em here!" added the watchman to the girl, who speedily started upon her errand.

With the aid of the watchman; Mr. Precise now carried poor Lize up stairs, and at her earnest prayer bore her into the room where Angelina was laying. He saw the handle of the knife which was in her breast, and was about to draw it out, when she cried :

"No, don't take it out yet, my life will go with it, and I'm dying fast enough now! Raise me up so that I can see my cousin!"

"They did so. There lay the poor sewing-girl, pale as snow, and alas, full as cold. Her eyes were unclosed—but with a dim glaze they were turned toward the door-way, as if she had been looking for some one to enter. Her hands were crossed upon her breast, and that breast was motionless.

"My God, she is dead!" groaned Mr. Precise, reaching forward and taking hold of one of her small, thin hands.

"Dead!" shrieked Lize, "*Dead!* Without one parting look or word for me! Oh, God, I could have died easier to have spoken one word to the blessed angel!"

"She was living when I went down stairs!" said the old man, while the hot tears rained down his cheeks. "I didn't think she could go off so soon. Jenny and me were sitting by her, talking to her, when we heard you scream!"

The watchman turned his face away from the scene—but it was only to hide the tears which also coursed down his weather-beaten cheeks.

"Raise me up—lay me on the bed by her side—she's dead now and wont mind the blood!" said Lize, faintly, "I want to kiss her—oh, God, why couldn't she be spared when there's so many sinners on earth!"

They laid the wounded woman upon the same bed. How could they refuse her dying request. In a few moments more the doctor, and other watchmen came. While the police were engaged in looking at the damage below, and were seeing what the robbers had done, the doctor looked at the wound of Lize. He saw in a moment that she could not live, and told her so, adding that her time was very brief.

"I'm contented to go," she murmured, "now that poor Angy has gone—but there's two things trouble me very much!"

"What are they?" cried Mr. Precise. "Anything I can do for you I will!"

"One of them you can—the other it's too late to think of!"

replied the unhappy woman. "If you can find my poor old
father and help him along, do it, for God's sake! He hasn't long
to live—he's very old and shackly!"

"If I can find him, he shall want for nothing!" said Mr. Precise, "and I wont rest till I do find him! But what was that
other wish of yours?"

"That I might go to heaven with Angy!" groaned Lize, burst-
ing into tears; "but I know it's no use for me to think of that—I've
been too bad—too hellish bad! Oh, God, have mercy on me!"

Both Mr. Precise and the doctor wept, and the latter in a
kindly tone said,

"A death-bed is a bad place for repentance, my poor woman;
yet with our merciful God there is forgiveness even at this
hour!"

"Oh, God, no! None for me—such a miserable sinner!"
groaned the wretched creature.

"Christ forgave the dying thief upon the cross!" urged the
good-hearted physician.

The woman shook her head hopelessly, and then bidding Mr.
Precise listen to her, told him of the plan for the robbery, how
she had been confined, had dug her way out of the cellar, and
then had reached his house, not in time to prevent the robbery,
but only to meet her death in the attempt.

The old man listened in silent suprise.

"Francis didn't come home last night—all must be true!" he
muttered, when she had finished, "and yet I thought he was
such a good boy and loved his mother so!"

The watchman now came up and begged Mr. Precise to go
down and see what he had lost, and leaving the doctor with
the wounded woman for a moment, he did so. His little safe
had been broken open, its contents were gone, as also sundry
articles of plate, wearing apparel, &c. The thieves, however,
had been hurried off too soon to make as large a collection as
they intended.

But Mr. Precise seemed to care very little for his pecuniary
losses. His troubles up stairs called him back, and he again
hurried to the side of the dead and dying.

Poor Lize was writhing in the last agony of her wound, listening to a few hasty words of instruction and comfort from the lips of the excellent doctor, who seemed, unlike too many of his profession, to think the soul worth caring for, as well as the body.

Who have better chances for doing moral good—what classes of men is there who can do more good with true piety, than the medical profession—men who are daily and nightly called to the bed side of the sick and dying; who meet their fellow-mortals in those hours when death and a future world being close before them, they *must* think of their soul's welfare.

When Mr. Precise again took the hand of Lize she was weakening very fast.

"Raise me up once more!" she said, "I *must* bend over and kiss poor Angy's lips again! She is an angel—oh, God, if I could but hope to see her in another world!"

It was a piteous sight to see that dying woman cling to the dead girl's form, and press her lips upon the pale, cold brow.

"I wish I could be laid in the same grave!" she murmured.

"You shall—you've been a brave, noble friend to her and me!" said Mr. Precise, in broken sobs.

"No, no!" murmured the poor woman—"you mus'n't do it. She is too good and pure. Bury me near her, but not with her; she is an angel—and I—oh, God, what a sinner I am!"

Neither Mr. Precise or the doctor could speak. The scene was too affecting. Lize, however, gathered strength by a moment's rest, and then said:

"Bury her and me in the lower corner, back from the street, of —— church yard. My mother is buried there—her aunt. I was there yesterday—no, 'twas the day before, I believe. I was there to look for my father. Bury us there, but don't put us in one grave, poor Angy is too good to lay alongside o' me!"

"Everything you wish shall be done," sobbed Mr. Precise.

"Do hunt up my poor old father!" added the woman. "Do hunt him up, and keep him from suffering!"

"So help me God, I will!" said Mr. Precise, fervently.

"Then I've no more to ask. One kiss more, dear Angy!"

She raised herself alone with a convulsive effort, and again kissed the brow of her dead cousin, and took a long look at her thin but beautiful features.

"Do shut up her eyes!" she murmured. "Let me see 'em closed before I go off!"

The doctor complied with her request, and then the woman kissed her lips, ice cold as they were, once again passionately. She then turned her eyes to Mr. Precise, and in a low tone, said,

"God bless you, sir, you was very good to *her!* She'll say a good word for you up above, I know she will!"

Mr. Precise sobbed all the harder while she spoke.

"Don't cry, sir," she said, "it's no use. 'T wont call *her* back, and it won't stop me from ——"

A groan burst from her lips and stopped her utterance, for the death pangs were upon her.

"Good bye!" she murmured, to Mr. Precise and the doctor, "good bye, gal," she added, to Jenny, who stood sobbing at the foot of the bed, "good bye, and don't lead sich a life as I have!"

Then she seized the hilt of the knife which still remained in her side, and murmuring, "God have mercy on my soul," drew it out, and died in an instant.

Her last breath was a prayer for mercy. She was a repentant, despairing, yet a pleading sinner. May we not hope for a better fate than eternal misery for her? She had many and grievous faults; yet she had virtues, warm and noble impulses.

We will finish the history of her and hers in this chapter. When on the next day Mr. Precise went to the burying ground which she had named, to make arrangements for the burial, he learned that the dead body of an old man had been found on a grave, in the corner of the grave-yard, which she had described, and on going to the coroner's office, found that it answered the description which Lize had given of her father, and some papers with his name, Robert Lindsay, on them, satisfied him of the identity of the wretched old man. He had died upon the grave of his wife—died without knowing that his unhappy daughter was to lie by his side in the same grave.

The three were buried, and Mr. Precise caused their graves to be enclosed carefully with an iron railing. Above the grave of Angelina, he had a plain white marble stone raised, with no name upon it, but a winged and smiling angel was sculptured on the snow-white stone. And while he shed tears over her grave, he gave the old sexton some money, and told him to plant flowers there as soon as the spring time came on.

CHAPTER IX.

Mrs. Abingdon made her arrangements for another visit to Genlis, according to the directions of her husband, and after night-fall, at the usual hour, proceeded to Julia's to meet the carriage.

Mr. Abingdon had already started for the same place, in company with his friend M—— and a large posse of policemen, who were to be secreted in the neighborhood, ready to act when called upon.

This time the driver of the hack occupied but a few moments in taking her to her destination—not necessitated to use the "round about" method any more.

Upon her arrival, he gave the usual signal, and she was led through the same winding ways as before, and finally seated, as she supposed, in the room where she had before met Genlis.

She heard his voice a moment afterward, close by her side.

"For what have you again come to us?" he asked. "Have you determined to pay the sum I demanded? Am I to take the journey for the child?"

"I know not what to say or do!" replied Mrs. A. "If you would let me tell my husband——"

"Why, he'd go and consult with some magistrate, and try to get me in trouble! I know what *men* are, well enough. No, no, you must keep my secret to yourself!" replied the Gipsey.

"But you will let me see the picture once more, will you not?"

"Yes, if you so desire it. But 'tis of little use, you have seen it once, and we can show you no more!"

"Then let me once more look upon the same scene!" said Mrs. A. "You cannot dream how I love that boy—he was named after a dear and noble brother of mine, who is seeking fame and fortune far beyond the ever-heaving sea ;—do let me again look upon the picture !"

" You shall !" said the Gipsey.

He then left her for a few moments, and she plainly heard whispering in the upper end of the room. He soon returned, and saying to her :

" Be silent and behold !" took off the shawl which had been bound over her eyes.

The same beautiful figure was kneeling by the curtain, and when Genlis waved his wand the curtain rose, as if moved by magic, and the mirror with its rolling mists appeared as before.

When the mists cleared away, Mrs. A. again saw her child, but once more the picture was changed. The child was in a kneeling posture, his little hands crossed upon his bosom, and his sweet face turned toward a clouded and troubled sky.

The back ground was dim and misty ; the boy was surrounded by a kind of fog, which rendered even his figure dim and vague. ·

The curtain had been up scarce a moment, when a slight noise behind him caused Genlis to turn quickly, and he beheld the magistrate and Mr. Abingdon enter the room.

" Curse you, you have betrayed me ! You shall never see your child again !" he cried, bitterly, darting a fiery look at Mrs. A. Then rushing toward the curtain, which dropped instantly, he cried to the person who knelt by it,

" Back, Inez, back to the trap—quick, or we'll be nabbed !"

Both himself and the woman sprung behind the curtain, and though Mr. M—— and Mr. Abingdon hurried to the spot and tore down the curtain in a moment, Genlis and his wife had disappeared. Word was quickly passed to the police outside, and a careful watch kept, but no more was seen of Genlis or his wife.

The *magic* of their operations, however, was at once discovered. The mirror, a large plate of glass lined on the inner side with a thin sheet of common white wax, was connected with a very ingenious contrivance, which consisted of a small steam boiler, set in the cellar below, which could convey a current of steam or heated air to the wax in the back of the mirror rendering it transparent. Through this, whatever pictures, or figures they chose to introduce behind the glass could be seen, and when they wished to dim, or destroy the effect, they had only to apply a current of cold air, blown by a large bellows from an ice-chest also placed in the cellar.

The contrivance was very ingenious, as figures seen through the glass, looked precisely as if they were shown upon the face of a mirror, and the distance at which the deluded visitors were kept, of course prevented them from seeing any small inaccuracies.

Mr. Genlis had apparently done a very large business, for the police found an immense number of lay figures, masks, wigs, dresses and paintings, which had undoubtedly been used to dupe different customers, who came to read their fortunes in the " Magic glass."

We have no doubt but that some of the readers of this book may have been to see this same Genlis, if so they will at once comprehend how natural and simple was the arrangement which they then thought so supernatural. And here, better than any where else, we can say a word to the ignorant and deluded, don't be offended, but we must say, *weak-minded* persons, who are daily crowding to visit pretended fortune-tellers in this city. There are no less than thirty-seven persons in New York, who are engaged in duping credulous sewing-girls, servants and others, into a belief that they have a knowledge of the future, which, for a good portion of their hard earned wages, they are willing to tell. They openly advertise their villainous humbuggery—and the worst of it all, is, that nearly all of these pretended fortune-tellers, are *procurers* for houses of ill-fame, wretches employed by kindred demons to fill the gardens of vice and iniquity with fresh flowers, as fast as the old ones decay or die off.

It is time, more than time, that the city government looked into this matter. Is there not a law to punish them as vagrants or disorderlies? If there is not, there should be, for these fortune-tellers consort with, and abet thieves, and every class of villains in the city.

And they make fortunes, absolutely *fortunes*, in their trade of lying, humbuggery and deception. They will take fifty cents or a dollar, the earnings of a whole week's labor, from a poor girl, then after fumbling over a pack of dirty cards, or looking at pretended Astrological tables, they will tell her about some "dark *complected* man," whiskered and moustached, who is to come "over water" to wed her—tell her of carriages and liveries, and so excite the imagination of the young creature, that she is no more fit to work, and is left in an unhappy state of expectation until ruin overtakes her.

The city should be cleared of these *pests ;*—it is a pity that so far as they are concerned, the old Salem "blue laws" could not be revived.

Any man, woman or child, of common sense, with one grain of reasoning power, must know that their pretended arts are all delusions, and we scarce know whether most to pity or condemn the people who will continue to be deluded by them, and who not only support them in their infamous trade, but aid in making them rich, while the imposters laugh at them, when their backs are turned.

Some of these wretches use mesmerism in their trade—others, blasphemous, sacrilegious *fiends,* dare to use the holy name of *religion* as a cloak to their satanical doings! But enough of them for the present. We will return to our story.

The magistrate and Mr. Abingdon were soon satisfied that Genlis had either stolen, or been connected with the thieves who stole little Willie, for the child's clothes were discovered upon a little lay figure, which was *faced* with a mask painted to resemble him, and surmounted by curls of the same color as his own hair. It was no wonder then that at a distance, through thick plate glass, and the transparent wax, the excited mother should think that she recognized her child. The clothes were the same he had worn at his disappearance.

Though they soon discovered how Genlis, his wife and their assistants had escaped, they could learn nothing of the child. The fortune-telling gang, had been prepared for any interruption, for a passage from their cellar was opened through into a little shop in the street back of their house, which was kept by one of their gang, and all easily made their escape before any efforts could be used to intercept them. Even the person of whom they rented the house, had not known their business or arrangements, so quietly and secretly had all been conducted.

His tenants had paid their rent regularly, and that was all that he cared for. Like some of our real estate owners in this city, who, though *professing* to be pious men, actual members of christian churches—rent houses for the purposes of prostitution; who actually own well known houses of ill-fame; he never *personally* inspected the place, but was satisfied that his tenants should call upon him and pay him his quarterly dues.

Mr. and Mrs. Abingdon were now in a worse fix than ever. They knew that their child, if still living, was in the power of a desperate and profligate crew, and they had good reason to fear that it might now be killed in revenge. The warm-hearted and excellent magistrate could do no more for them than he had; they had no remedy or hope, except to continue the search for their child; or to recover him by the offer of a large reward.

They took possession of the picture of the school-room, and the little village, in hopes that it might lead them upon some clue to their child, and Mr. A. also determined to give up house-keeping, and to commence travelling through the country in search of the boy.

On the very same night that the house of Genlis was broken up, the dwelling of Mr. A. was entered by burglars, and every dollar of ready money, all his plate, &c. carried away. The robbers did their job so neatly and well, that they did not even disturb Mr. A. and his wife, or the servants, though they had to open an iron safe, and several doors, which had been left locked and bolted when the family retired to rest.

CHAPTER X.

It was not late—not more than nine in the evening, when Charles Meadows started to go to the room of Harry Whitmore, attended by Mose and his party. But as they came near the C—— House, they observed a large crowd was assembled around it.

"Wonder if it's a fire?" said Mose—"the old bell aint a chimin', and I don't hear the forty's out!"

"No, it's no fire!" said Meadows, with a shudder. "There's not enough noise, about it!"

He knew but too well the cause of that collection of people, and we can only wonder that he dared to approach that spot— that he had the hardihood, as he did, to enter the very room where the dead man lay, and to look upon his ghastly face. And that was the *first* time he had ever seen it. Carlton had not told him who was the man that he wished killed—the victim had been led to him in the dark, and, blindly, madly, he had slain him.

Mose had entered with Charles, anxious to know what the muss was.

"Why, Charley!" he cried, as soon as he looked at the corpse, " darned if this 'ere isn't Charley Cooly, our old school-mate!"

Meadows gazed one moment, then hiding the horrible sight from his eyes with his hands, heaved a deep and heavy groan, one that fairly startled the bystanders.

"Poor feller! Charley's mighty sorry an' so 'm I! If I know'd who did this, I'd *lam* him—I'd lam him 'till he couldn't say a prayer!" cried Mose.

Meadows turned away—he could not bear to take another glance at the corpse. He had indeed slain an old friend and school-mate—one who in boyhood had joined in the same sports, had even helped him to learn his hard lessons; for Cooly was several years his senior.

As he turned away, he said to Mose, "Stay down here, or out at the door, till I go up and see this Whitmore."

"No, can't stand that, no way!" said the warm-hearted fellow; "S'pose you should get inter a muss up there! I must go alo—ong!"

"Well, have it so, if you will; but don't bring up the whole party!"

"No, I wont," replied Mose. "Sykesey, stan' to the door, you an' the rest o' the b'hoys, till me and Charley comes down; but mind, if you hear me yelp, you jist come right *in!*"

"We wont do nothin' shorter, hoss!" replied Sykesey, and with this assurance, Mose and the clerk went up stairs to the room of Livingston, where, as the reader is already aware, Whitmore lay.

There was a party of young men in the room. They were seated around a centre-table, upon which stood sundry bottles of wine. The young *gentlemen* were engaged in "a friendly game of poker," which did not appear to be "entirely for amusement," as considerable change lay in small heaps around the board.

On a couch, or French sofa, near the table, engaged in watching the players, lay Whitmore. His head was still bound up, and his arm was in splints, so that he could not join in the amusement. Livingston was amongst the players, as also a hungry-looking, hatchet-faced individual, whose countenance resembled that of a young opossum very much, who was known to his comrades as *the* "Count 'Lijah."

The gentlemen started to their feet, as Meadows and Mose entered, and stared strangely, especially at the latter, not knowing what to make of the intrusion.

Whitmore turned slightly pale for a moment, but quickly recovered his self-possession, and said, with a smile,

"Ah, how d'ye do, Charley? Glad to see you! Gentlemen, my friend, Mr. Meadows!"

"I wish to have a moments private conversation with you,

sir, before I permit you to use the title of *friend* to *me !*" said the clerk, sternly.

"Certainly, sir! certainly! Mr. Livingston just take your party out into the next room, for a moment, if you please. Charley has some business with me!" replied Whitmore, perfectly calm in outward looks, though his very heart was frozen as he faced the injured brother, who looked so changed, so ghastly pale, from the excitement through which he had passed that evening.

"By the piper what played afore Moses and the bull-rushes—that's the feller I gived *jessy* to, last night!" said Mose, aside. "He'll not want to stick a B'howery b'hoy, afore soon agin!"

The young gentlemen left the room, as requested by Whitmore, who looked at Mose after they had left, and then, glancing at Meadows, asked:

"Do you wish that young man to remain?"

"He don't want nothin' else!" said Mose, gruffly; "an' if he did, he couldn't help his self."

"Well, Sir, I will hear your *business*, if business has brought you here. I thought you'd come to *see* a sick friend, merely. I was knocked into a cocked hat by some infernal rascal last night!"

"Lookee here, hoss-fly, if you say that 'ere agin, I'll have to do su'thin' that goes aginst my grain; I'll have to lam a man that's on his back a'ready! I lammed you last night—an' I aint no rascal, and that's more'n you can say for yourself!" cried Mose, starting forward to the bed-side of Whitmore, and shaking his huge fist in the invalid's face.

"Don't strike him, Mose, he's got some questions to answer to me!" said Meadows, drawing back the young butcher.

"I aint agoin' to hit him, Charley!" replied the latter, "but I don't like to be called hard names, by nobody, and it makes me mussy!"

"Well, Mr. Meadows, what questions have you to ask?" said Whitmore, who had begun to flush up a little, at the rather uncomplimentary language of honest Mose.

"Where is my sister?" asked Meadows, sternly eyeing the young man.

"Your sister !" echoed Whitmore ; "isn't she at home ?"

"No, Sir, you *know* she is not !" said Meadows, sternly.

"I do not know any such thing !" replied Whitmore ; "I got a message from my sister, early this morning, saying that her aunt had sent for her up the river, being suddenly taken ill, and that she had to start off in the morning boat. She said your sister had gone home. I hope nothing has happened to her !"

"Gass ! He's a stuffin' you, Charley !" said Mose, indignantly.

"Then you say you know nothing of my sister's whereabouts ? Will you *swear* it ?" asked Meadows.

"I *will*—so help me God, I haven't seen her since early last evening, just before I met you, and I got into the difficulty soon after, which has left me here helpless, as you see me !" replied Whitmore, earnestly.

"My God ! I know not what to do, or what to make of this affair !" groaned Meadows.

"What is the matter, Meadows, *do* tell me ?" said Whitmore, in an earnest tone. "Has anything happened to Miss Meadows ? For God's sake tell me !"

"He cannot know anything of it !" muttered the clerk, completely deceived by the dissembling villain.

"Speak—for Heaven's sake, tell me, has any harm befallen her ?" continued Whitmore, still more earnestly. "If there has, tell me—I claim a right to know, even by the feelings which she and I have entertained for each other !"

"He cannot know it—he cannot be guilty !" again muttered Meadows, to himself, and then he replied to the young man.

"She has not come home yet, and we are very much alarmed for her safety !" said Charles, unwilling to let Whitmore know the extent of his fears, and fully satisfied that he at least was innocent.

"My God, what can have detained her. This is such a villainous place—I wish that I could get about to aid you in your search for her—your friend there did a bad job when he laid me out !" said Whitmore, in a kind and feeling tone.

"Maybe, I did !" said Mose. "But you shouldn't ha' drawn your sticker on me. If you'd hit me with your fist like a man,

I'd sarved you out with the same tools, and you'd got off with a black eye, or some other little peculiar mark o' mine ; but when you drawed your weapon, I was bound to haul out mine, you know. But if Charley here's satisfied that you ha'n't done nuthin' wrong, I don't mind sayin' I'm sorry, an' makin' on it up with you ! Will you gi's your hand ?"

"Yes, certainly. I have good reasons on my side, for saying that I'm sorry for *our* difficulty !" replied Whitmore, shaking the hand of Mose, and at the same time glancing at his own splintered arm.

"Well, better luck next time, as the g'hal said when she got a bad husband !" replied Mose, then turning to Meadows, he added :

"I say Charley, ha'n't you got nothin' agin them fellers that sloped into t'other room ?"

"No," replied Meadows, "I have not."

"Then aren't we agoin' to have a muss after all ?"

"No," said the clerk. "There is no necessity for it !"

"Then I'm mighty sorry—ha'n't had no muss, 'cept a little blow out last night, for ever so long—a'most a whole week. An' fires is so uncommon scarce, jist now—a plug muss is *rich* —I like to go in when I'm at a fire, jist to keep cool !"

"Let us go. I must continue the search," said Meadows.

"Well, I'll go lo-ong ; but I'm so sorry we can't git a muss !" said Mose. "There was one of them ar fellers what went into t'other room, look sarcy at me, jist as if he thought I'd buy dead hogs and sell 'em for fresh pork, when they'd died 'cordin' to onnateral nater, without being stuck, and hung up like decent pigs is ! I wonder if he didn't want a muss, if he did, he'd only have to say so !"

"Oh, they were all peaceable. They didn't mean to look saucy at you !" said Whitmore.

"Well, if so be you say so, since we're friends, I'll let it slide !" said Mose, "but how I could lam him, or any other *he* to-night. Charley if we don't find 'Bell to-night, I'm bound to raise a muss somewhere !"

"Then I expect, you'll *have* to raise a muss," said Whitmore, as the two disappeared, " for my plans are laid a little too well,

36

to be foiled easily.   "Old Ma'am S. knows her business well—
and in a few days, I shall be about.   I wont be caught quite as
easy as that fool Cooly, who lies below stairs now, a victim to
his own carelessness.   I don't blame a man half so much for
getting into a love scrape, as I do for getting caught at it !"

"Have you got clear of him ?" asked Livingston, entering the
room.

"Of *course* I have !" said Whitmore, proud of his success.

"But didn't he suspect you ?"

"No, devil the bit.   I came the sympathetic and all that over
him, and he has gone away to look for his sister, convinced that
I know nothing about her.   But I'll tell you what I wish you'd
do for me, Gus. !"

"What ?"

"Why, go 'round to the old woman's in Church street and see
how the girl gets along !"

"I've just come from there—I ran around while they were
talking to you, and found out that they'd been there already
But they couldn't make anything out of the old woman, she was
too keen for them !"

"But where was the girl.   Didn't they search the house ?"

"Yes, but Ma'am S. had found out that they were coming,
and stowed her away in the vault or coal-hole, I believe !"

"Good !   But what did she tell them ?"

"Why, she said that *a* Miss Meadows *had* been there with a
foreigner—a Spaniard or a Frenchman, she thought, and that
she went away with him again about noon to-day !"

"Better yet !   why, the old woman is a regular trump.   I'll
give her an extra hundred for that.   She must manage to get
the girl to her up town private house for me now, there'll be no
danger there, for the house is not much known ; and, besides, it
is well arranged for such matters.   She's told me some strange
yarns about the house ; and if the back-yard was dug into a
little ways, it's my private opinion that something strange would
be found.   *She* didn't exactly tell me so, but I found it out, and
I don't believe she'd like to see a spade put into ground there !"

"Why, what do you mean ?"

"Oh, nothing much. But there are easy ways of getting money, you know—and the ground is very convenient sometimes to put meat under, which might smell bad if kept above it—but, hush, there comes the Count and the rest of 'em. Never say anything about this matter—I got it from one of her girls when she was drunk!"

CHAPTER XI.

ANOTHER day had dawned. Mr. Shirley sat at his breakfast-table with their young and beautiful daughter, Constance.

The latter looked unusually well—her cheeks were as rosy as ever, her eyes as bright, but she noticed that both her parents looked pale, sick and care-worn.

She asked them repeatedly, if they were ill, but they told her they were not, and she was left to wonder what could be the matter.

Her father did not even take the Herald up, which the servant had laid beside his plate, though it had formerly been his habit to read the paper always at the breakfast-table.

On this morning it was laid within the reach of Constance, and seeing that her father did not touch it, she took it up and commenced reading.

The mother saw her daughter's cheeks flush up a moment after she took up the paper, and noticed that while she read eagerly on, her hand trembled with the paper, and her quick breathing denoted an unusual excitement.

"What is the matter, my child?" she asked, "what excites you so?"

"Oh, mother, here is an account of such a horrible affair!" replied the girl. "It makes my blood run cold to read it!—What dreadful fiends there are upon this earth!"

"What is it?" asked the mother.

"Why, mother, a poor girl's body has been found in the water, and some of her clothes and marks of a struggle, have been found close by the spot at Hoboken, and the paper says some ruffians ruined her there by cruel force, and then threw her in the water! Oh, how horrible—how she must have suffered—I can't bear to think of it; and then her lover, a worthy young mechanic, has committed suicide! Oh, mercy, it is too horrible!"

The young girl burst into tears. Her warm young heart was full of sympathy, and as her imagination painted the sufferings of such a horrible death, her tears would come.

"Let me see the paper!" said Mr. Shirley.

He took it from his weeping child, and as his eye fell upon the paragraph, he started, and then turned pale as if death had stricken him. It was well his daughter was sobbing, and had bowed her head down upon the table, else she could not have failed to notice his agitation. His wife saw it, and silently reached over for the paper. He handed it to her, and she glanced at the paragraph.

It was too much for her. She felt that she could not command her feelings as he had done, and she rose and left the room. She did not say one word—yet there were volumes of reproach in her look as she turned to go from the room, and her glance from him to their daughter, told him that for her alone, the young, pure and beautiful pledge of their early love, she bore with his crime, his terrible wrong.

And how did he feel. If he could have recalled the past with the loss of an arm, an eye, and a leg, I believe he would gladly have done it. If there is a hotter hell in another world than was then burning in his own breast, God pity those who are condemned to it.

The paragraph which he had glanced at, was a long account, detailing the finding the body of Mary Sheffield, the beautiful "Cigar Girl," and of her supposed ill-treatment and murder by a gang of rowdies at Hoboken.

The story seemed very probable. A place was described where some of her torn garments were found, and where broken bushes, &c. bore the marks of a struggle having taken place; and then in a little slack eddy of the river, close by, her body was found, bearing the marks of violence.

There were marks of violence upon her, not inflicted by a "gang of rowdies," but by a hag, a she-devil, an abortion of her own sex, one whom it would be blasphemy to call a *woman,* Caroline L. Sitstill.

Her plan was perfectly arranged. Everything *appeared* to have happened just as the paper stated—but never could the law or its keen-sighted officers find one of " the rowdies," who were *supposed* to have performed the horrible deed.

Of course not. The *abortionist* was the rowdy. Herself and two assistants had conveyed the body there—had placed the clothing where it was found, and all of this was done at the dead of night. And she got *one thousand dollars* for the "job."

But that is not a priming to the load reserved for her in another world. She has not only this victim to answer for, but *hundreds* of others, and her crimes must sink her so deep into the black waves of eternal misery, that all the prayers of every saint in heaven, if joined together into a lever, couldn't pry her out in the space of an eternity.

MURDERESS OF INNOCENTS ! PANDER OF INFAMY ! HAG OF HELL ! we can find no name black enough, sufficiently comprehensive of fiendishness, to class thee by. To rot in a dungeon, neck deep in filth, to have your food shared by rats, and your drink lapped from your very lips, by hissing snakes, should be your fate on earth. For the next world, you are well provided ; fear not, there's a warm berth waiting for you !

CHAPTER XII.

THE continued search for Isabella was in vain. Charles Meadows returned to his mother's house at a very late hour, almost delirious with excitement, and found her sick in bed, with a burning fever, raving about her children and the misery which seemed all at once to be settling down upon her hitherto happy household.

When Charles came in and found her thus, he would have instantly went for a doctor, but he dared not, for her ravings were of the murder, as well as her daughter's supposed abduction and disgrace, and he feared that his own crime might be exposed.

When she saw him, her first inquiry was for her daughter.

"Have you found poor 'Bell?" she asked, in a tone of blended anxiety and agony of suspense.

"No, no! I have heard of her, but cannot find her!" said the wretched brother.

"Had she been there in that terrible house, as the young man said?"

"Yes, and went away with her seducer, *willingly*, I heard!" groaned the clerk.

"Then may God curse her!" shrieked the mother, "if she has brought disgrace upon my grey hairs, if she has forgotten the lessons which I have taught her, may God Almighty bend down in his wrath and *curse* her!"

"Mother! mother! Do not rave so wildly. I do not know this, I only fear it! I heard it from a *thing* who trades in the virtue, no, in the vice of her sex, as butchers deal in meat, and regards women according to their youth and fat, alone, as a butcher does the drove which he buys for his slaughter-house!"

" And *she*—my daughter, has been there in the power of this woman ?"

" Yes, yes !" rejoined the clerk, with a groan.

" Then *she* is blasted for ever ! Now for *you !*" rejoined the mother, sitting up in her bed, and glaring at him with strange looks, such as she never had given him before. " You, Charles, are a *murderer ?* Speak ! is it not so ?"

The young man blanched before her steady gaze. His lips quivered—his form shook, cold drops of clammy sweat oozed out upon his brow.

" I was a fool to tell you !" he muttered—" I ought to have kept it to myself !"

" Could you have kept it from *God ?*" she shrieked, " No, no ! Your hand is red with the blood of your fellow-man—go forth— go forth, I say, and leave the widow desolate ! Son, daughter, both gone—for ever gone !"

"Mother, for Heaven's sake calm yourself !" implored the son.

" You'll rouse the neighbors—they will know our disgrace ; for God's sake be calm !"

" Yes, I'll be calm, very calm ! I'm going to die—I'm going up to God, where you may *never* come !" continued the mother, in the same wild tone. And then she added :

"Don't you bury me, Charles, your hand is red ; and don't let 'Bella come and weep over my grave, for her soul is dark now !"

" Mother, Mother, don't talk so, or I shall go mad !" groaned the clerk.

"Go mad ?" she shrieked, " and wherefore not ? Murder is madness, and you're a murderer ! Ha ! I see a snake twined 'round your forehead—the dream, the *dream !*"

With a prolonged and terrible shriek, the wretched widow fell back senseles, on her bed. Charles thought she was dead. He could not revive her, and careless of risk hastened out for a doctor.

The doctor came, and after hours of exertion, brought her back to consciousness. But Charles had now no reason to fear that she would divulge his dreadful secret. She was a moping, speechless idiot. Her reason had fled for ever. Her troubles had been too heavy for her strength of mind.

Oh, who can picture the remorse of that son, when he saw the wreck before him. This living murder sunk his *last* crime into insignificance, his heart was a very hell of remorse! Why did he live—why did he not now try the poison, or the deadly steel? Crime had made him a coward, and he dared not! He feared to face the unknown terrors of another world.

A ruined sister—a maniac mother—and to himself he ascribed all the blame. Had I not, he argued, gone to the gaming table, I should never have introduced my sister to acquaintances which would have led her out, and into consequent danger; had I not gamed, I should never have been placed in the power of Carlton, the fiend in human guise!

Thus he blamed himself—but even then he did not go to the root of the evil. If he had not been first duped, and led into a gambling house, by a gambler's genteel outside assistant, he never would have gamed; had the authorities of the city done *their* duty, and suppressed gambling here, he never could have been led astray, therefore, we will charge, as the *principal* and first cause of the murder, and all of this wretchedness and ruin, the neglect of the city authorities in doing their *duty!* They were *really* the *criminals*—they permitted the villains to dupe an innocent victim; they winked at the open law breaking, as they do now, or else they did as the custom-house officers do with smugglers in Cuba, looked at the criminals through a pair of very thick golden spectacles. We have no other way left us to judge of their conduct. They receive certain salaries to do their duty, and they must be paid better to neglect it.

I charge the misery of every man who is ruined at a gaming table in New York, and the consequent misery of his family, to the *authorities* of this city. If in despair he commits suicide, *they* are his *murderers;* for they permit, and in so doing, abet the open keeping of gambling houses.

The moral citizens of this town have borne this system of things long enough. Another year the *elections* will tell the *recreants* to their duty that we are waking up. If it is in the power of our pen to point out the delinquents, and to trace their abettings in, or winkings at crime, we will do it—with a free hand, careless whether we offend *persons* or not, so long as we are doing *our* duty ! If they will not do *their* duty, ours shall not be neglected, nor will we stand idle, and see the city overrun with " Peter Funks," " Gamblers," " Fortune-tellers," " murderers," " abortionists" and other thieves and wretches, who openly pursue their horrible trades, without at least raising our voice against them.

CHAPTER XIII.

WHEN Charles Meadows found that his mother's case was hopeless, and that his sister's fate could not be ascertained, he determined to leave the country. On a plea of the sickness of his mother, he had managed for two days to be excused from attendance at his employer's store, and now on the second night after the murder, he repaired to Carlton's house to see him.

What was his astonishment upon meeting the gambler to find himself treated very coldly.

"What is your wish, Mr. Meadows—what can I do for you this evening?" said the gambler, who received the clerk in his private room.

"Money—sir! Money to leave this cursed town!"

"How much, sir; we are very short just now; how much do you want?"

"All you promised me!" replied the clerk, gruffly.

"My promise was made at a moment of great excitement, Mr. Meadows," said the gambler, coolly, "and I am now very short of funds—if five hundred dollars will be of any use to you, why I have it at your service!"

"Five hundred devils!" shouted the clerk. "Scoundrel do you mean to insult me?"

"No, not at all, Mr. Meadows, but you use harsh terms in addressing a gentleman!"

"Do you mean to pay my demands? I want all—every cent you promised me!"

"You cannot have it, sir. I have already given you seventeen thousand, eight hundred and fifty dollars!"

"Liar! You, yourself told me that the money you gave me was counterfeit!" cried the clerk.

"Yes, I *told* you so, but it was to keep you in hand while I wanted you. The money was good, or old S—— would have found it out before now !"

" Villain ! Had I known that before, I would have cut my right hand off before l would have done what I have for you !"

" Knowing that, of course, I was bound not to tell you !" · said the gambler, with a sneer, and then he added, " if you have any more to say, say it quick, I am waited for below !"

" I want five thousand dollars, to-night !" said the clerk.

" You can't have it !" replied Carlton, firmly.

" Then, by heaven, I'll expose you—-I'll let out the whole affair of the murder !"

" Thereby putting your own neck into the halter, without endangering me in the least; for you cannot *prove* anything against me, you could not be a witness, and there is no other !"

" Your wife, sir !"

" My wife !" laughed the gambler. " Are you such an ignoramus as not to know that a wife cannot be a witness against her husband ? Go ahead, hang yourself, if you will, but you can't hurt me—I *defy* you !"

The maddened clerk knew that this was but too true. He groaned in his misery, and dashed his clenched hand against his burning brow.

" Curse you ! Curse you !" he cried, " you have damned me for ever, and now you glory in it. If I could draw you into the same disgrace and destruction, I'd die a felon's death with joy !"

" Fortunately, you cannot !" said the gambler, with a sneer. " But dropping that unpleasant subject, do you not intend to retain your situation with S——? You are square with him now, you can turn honest, and I advise you not to play any more. You're bound to lose if you play with sporting men. *Luck* is all gammon, where they're in the game !"

" I shall go there no more—I dare not !" groaned the clerk. " For God's sake, Carlton, give me five thousand and let me leave the country !"

" I'm sorry, but on my honor I haven't the amount !" replied the gambler. " As I said before, I can spare five hundred, but I cannot do more !"

" Give it to me !" gasped the clerk. " I cannot leave the country with it, but I can live upon it for a while, till I can get another place, for I will *not* go back to S."

The gambler counted out the money.

"There," said he, handing it to the clerk, " there is the amount. Now let me caution you not to bet at faro any more, or you'll lose it. You can't win—I tell you as a *friend*, you *can't* win !"

"*As a friend.*" God save men from such friends as *Henry Carlton*—God save them from any of his fiendish, unprincipled clan.

Meadows took the money and left the house of the wretch who had ruined him, left it a desperate, remorseful, almost broken-hearted man.

He had been deceived by his betrayer—he had felt the keen sting of base ingratitude from the very man who had driven him to the most fearful of all crimes. He had learned a common lesson : that to win a man's enmity and hate, you must do him every favor in your power; peril your life and blast your very soul for him.

CHAPTER XIV.

A MONTH passes away very quickly doesn't it reader? Especially if you are happy, or if you have a great deal of work to do, which must be finished in a limited time, for instance, a long tale to write at a day's notice, or some other labor wherein you are expected to ao both yourself and your employer justice, without a moment for thought, study, or preparation.

But if you are on a sick-bed, how clogged are the wheels of time, how the minutes drag their " slow lengths" along.

How long must a month seem to a prisoner who is barred from the glad sunlight, whose very existence is wrapped in a cloud. Yet, if he be condemned to a felon's death, the moments must fly to him—they cannot, will not be tardy enough for his satisfaction.

If one has a note out, payable at thirty days from date, and money is scarce, time seems to work on the " telegraph" principle; if he has money *due* him, the contrary old wretch crawls along, as if he was trying not to beat a snail as hard as he could.

For myself (not that I have had notes out, or been so exceedingly happy), my whole life-time has been but as a short and fleeting dream; not one of sunshine and flowers, of music or of gladness, but of storm and tempest; of passion and excitement; wild, and rapid, and lonely as the single cloud, which by itself is borne along amidst the red lightnings on the winged gale, where the elements all meet and war with each other.

Forgive this self-allusion, friendly reader, it came all unconsciously out, like the Irishman's joke, and now that it is on paper, it would be a waste of ink to blot it out—the reader who *must* be witty at my expense, will add that 'twas a waste of ink to put it there.

A month has passed in our history—a month since we left one

of the purest and most interesting of all our characters, in peril and darkness. Would to God that we might record that she then and there had died, rather than be forced, as we are, to tell a history of misery and shame. We cannot tell it—our pen cannot trace the burning record of foul wrong. We can only hint at vile *drugs*, at the foul and villainous wrong of a wretch, who laid desolate as fair a flower of pure nature as ever was born on earth.

We must in these vague terms pass over the events of a month, and come to the following scene.

It is laid in the second-story back-chamber of a house up-town—a fine-looking dwelling, in the very centre of an *aristocratic* row of buildings in the most fashionable quarter of the city.

A female is seated on an elegant sofa in this chamber, gazing sadly, but quietly, out of the window, into a little flower-garden which is back of the house. Now and then, through the space left by an open lot, she looks over into a street beyond and notes the various passengers, and watches the gambols of sundry little children, who are rejoicing in the soft and balmy spring air.

Her cheek is pale and thin, and her eyes are red with continuous weeping, and even yet she is beautiful. A loose *robe de nuit* does not conceal the beauties of her voluptuous form. The very carelessness with which her luxuriant, dark brown curls, fall upon her neck, adds to their rich loveliness, and aids well to contrast the snowy whiteness of her neck.

She was alone in the elegantly furnished room. A guitar was cast down upon one end of the sofa ; books lay scattered round ; a toilet table, with its many luxuries, occupied a corner of the room.

To judge from appearances, she could not be in want of anything which art could devise, or wealth command.

And this was Isabella Meadows—no longer the pure-souled, high-principled incarnation of living virtue—but a lost and ruined girl. The house where we now exhibit her, was only a private palace of infamy, kept for a select few, by the wealthy hag, in whose den we last left the unfortunate girl.

We will not detail *how* poor Isabella became the tainted and blasted creature we now find her—it is enough—too much that we find her so.

We do not know what her thoughts were, as she sat there and gazed out of the window, but whatever they were, their chain was broken by the opening of the chamber door and the entrance of another of our well-known characters. He came in with a smile—*he*, the destroyer of that hapless creature, Henry Whitmore, entered with a *smile*.

His arm is yet in a sling, and he is slightly pale from his recent confinement.

And Isabella Meadows turns her eyes toward him, and with a sad smile greets him. Poor thing, she is endeavoring to bear up as well as she can—like the poor girl who was confined in the garret with her, she knows that she is ruined and cannot help herself.

"Well, 'Bella, how d' you get along?" said the young man, carelessly seating himself by her side, and throwing his arm over her lovely shoulder.

"Sadly, Harry," she replied ; "I'm very lonesome and unhappy when you are not here !"

"Then why don't you seek the society of the other girls ?"

"Oh, Harry, they are so coarse in their remarks. They are very vulgar and swear at every tenth word, almost !"

"Well, that's nothing. You'll get into it yourself, bye and bye !" replied the unfeeling wretch.

"Oh, God, no, I hope not !" said the girl, tearfully. "I know I am a lost and ruined creature, but I will not descend to blasphemy—I will not go deeper into sin than I am !"

"That be d——d. You'll soon be like all the rest—for all your preaching and soft talk now !"

"Harry, do not say that. You ought to pity me—for you have made me what I am !"

"There you are again, with your eternal rant about my ruining you, I do wish you'd sometimes change the subject !"

Isabella eyes flashed for a moment with the fire of anger.

"You do not like to hear the truth, sir !" she said, bitterly

"You do not like to have me recall your base and unmanly villainy !"

"Come, come, 'Bell, don't let's have another scene !" said the young man, a little more kindly.

"I did not wish to have a scene, as you call it, Henry, but by your unkindness you forced it upon me !"

"Well then, pass it over, I'm sorry if I was rough !" said Whitmore.

The kindly tone with which he uttered this, operated in a moment upon Isabella, and while tears came in her eyes, she said,

"Thank you—thank you, Harry, for that kind word. I never expect to be happy, but when you are unkind I grow desperate. Do not drive me to drink, do not force me into the vice and dissipation which I see around me. If I cannot be your *wife*, at least let me be as decent as I can !"

"Certainly,' Bell ; you are the prettiest woman in town, and I don't wonder that you wish to be exclusive. By the way, I owe some of my friends a supper party, I hope you'll not object to be present and do the honors !"

"Oh, Harry, *do* excuse me ! Is it not enough that *you* should know my degradation ? Do not make me a spectacle to your loose companions !"

"I don't wish to make you a spectacle, 'Bell ; they'd not know you, and a supper-party without a woman or two to enliven the scene is a dull affair ! You'll really do me a great favor if you'll attend this !"

"You shall have your way, Harry—but I shall be very unhappy when the eyes of strangers are upon me !"

"Oh, nonsense, 'Bell ! You'll not feel it after the first glance, and you are introduced to the company !"

"What note is that in your pocket ?" asked Isabella, glancing at a letter which had been carelessly thrust into his vest.

"Only an invitation to a party at a Mr. Shirley's !" replied the young man.

"What, the father of that beautiful young girl I met you walking with one day when we were first acquainted ?" asked the girl, flushing up a little.

"Yes, he's a merchant, and very well off !"

37

"Then you intend going to his party?" continued Isabella.

"Yes—I can't well get off. He's such a *particular* friend!"

A pang of jealousy shot through the unhappy girl's breast. She began to fear that he soon would desert her, even as a mistress, and she shuddered then at the dark and dreadful fate which awaited her—the life which she felt that she could not escape from.

"Have you seen my brother, to-day?" she continued, changing the subject of conversation.

"Yes," replied Whitmore, "I saw him, but he was very much flushed with liquor!"

"Alas, I am the cause of it!" said the unhappy girl.

"Oh, no, you are not. He has been dissipated for months. Before I knew you, he was at the gambling table every night. I was introduced to him at a place of that kind!"

"That was what kept him out so late, then?"

"Yes."

"And my mother—have you seen or heard of her?"

"She is up the river, with some friends, I hear, and is very comfortable, I believe!" replied the deceiver.

"Oh, I'm so glad of that. I expect she's with our relations in Hudson!" said the poor girl, little dreaming where and how her wretched mother really was.

"Does my brother suspect where I am, or how I'm living?" she continued.

"No, not where you are—but he thinks you've turned out, and are living with a Spaniard out of the city. Some one told him so. He has sworn to kill you, if he ever meets you!"

"Three weeks ago, I would have blessed him for the deed!" said she, with a sigh.

"And I, would not only have *cursed*, but would have shot him for it!" said Whitmore. "You were made for a better fate, 'Bell!"

"For a better fate!" she replied, in a sarcastic tone; "do you call the life I am leading now, a *better* fate? Henry Whitmore, so help me God, if I could recall the hour before I unconsciously took the draught which left me helpless, and in your power, and enabled you to make me what I am, I would destroy my own life, rather than live to be what I am. If I could be pure again, I would rather die than live !"

"Don't talk so, 'Bell. It's all very well for old maids to preach up such nonsense—but for you, who are so beautiful and so young, it is folly !"

"Folly or no folly, Harry, it is just as I feel. But I *am* what I am, now, and I cannot help it, only I pray you for my sake, aye, and for your own, not to do anything which will sink me deeper into degradation ! If I ever should get desperate, you would have to beware of me. There is a fiend in me, which must not be aroused !"

" Poh, 'Bell ! There's more of the angel in you, than the devil, a great deal !"

" No, Harry, all of the angel is *fallen*. I feel what I *am*—I tremble when I think what I may be !"

Reader, with the appendix which follows this chapter, we shall close this work. If you would follow the fate of Isabella Meadows, and see what a desperate, crime-hardened being a once pure and virtuous maiden may become, when driven to the very verge of madness, by ruin and wrong ; and if you would see the terrible retribution which followed the crime of Albert Shirley, and read a new and strange history in the fate of Constance, his lovely daughter, you must read

"THE B'HOYS OF NEW YORK,"

a work which will soon follow this, and which will also follow up the strange career of the two CARLTON's, SAM SELDEN, and other characters whom we have not disposed of in this work.

The work we can safely promise will be quite as thrilling, if not more so, than this, for we have wilder incidents, and stranger tales to tell, than the reader yet has seen.

The search of the Abingdon's after their child—after great expense and trouble, was at last rewarded with success. They found him at a village school, near Troy, where he had been placed by Genlis, who gave them information of his whereabouts, through an agent whom they paid handsomely for the **service.**

We subjoin a list of the characters, used in this work, which will find a place in the " B'hoys of New York."

Isabella Meadows,	Carlton and his wife,
Charles Meadows,	Sam. Selden & Co.,
Henry Whitmore,	Mose, Sykesey, & Co.,
Gus. Livingston,	Mr. Shirley, wife and daughter,
Count 'Lijah, and his set,	Ma'am S. & Co.

Also many new characters, drawn from real-life.

The author here also gives notice that he has secured the copy-right of the " G'hals of New York," another novel of an exciting character, already commenced, which will follow the first named in a short time.

He thanks his fellow-citizens for their *immense*, though he hopes, partially *deserved* patronage, and he assures them that he will endeavor to work up to his popularity, and keep his patrons supplied as long as they thus encourage him in his labors.

For a further view of his sentiments, &c., he refers to the following Appendix, which he requests his city readers, particularly *voters* and *tax-payers*, to notice.

Thanks—a thousand thanks for the unexpected and unprecedented favor with which this work has been received, and, kind patrons, receive my assurances that I'll try to do better next time.

NED BUNTLINE.

APPENDIX.

APPENDIX.

HAVING brought our story to a close, and, to the best of our ability, illustrated a few of the many mysteries and miseries of this city, we devote a few pages to a glance at the causes of the crime and vice which surround us.

In a letter from an esteemed correspondent, which we published in the Appendix to our third number, an allusion is made to a letter written by Wm. Cobbett, in 1818, wherein he speaks of the utter absence of crime in this city at that time, using the following language :

"New York itself contains nearly two hundred thousand inhabitants, and, after London, is the first commercial and maritime city in the world.—Thousands of sailors, ship-carpenters, dockyard people, cartmen, draymen, boatmen, &c. crowd its wharfs and quays. Yet never do we hear of a hanging; scarcely ever of a robbery ; men go to bed with scarcely locking their doors ; and never is seen in those streets what is called in England, a girl of the town, and what is still more, never is there seen in those streets a beggar. I wish you, my old neighbors could see this City of New York."

From an examination of the court records of that date, we find that Mr. C. made stronger representations of our city's purity than the *truth* would warrant, yet it is not to be denied that crime is now much more frequent than then ; that street begging now is systematized here, and that it is very necessary to "lock doors," and to use many other precautions against robbery.

From the "*Tribune*" of March 17th we take the following little list of arrests, which tells a rather different story from Cobbett's letter.

"During the month of February the following arrests were made by the Police of the City : for felony 5, burglary 9, suspicion of burglary 3, grand larceny 29, petit larceny 210, suspicion of larceny 47, receiving stolen goods 4, rape 4, suspicion of murder 2, lunatics 15, abandonment 4, infanticide 1, passing counterfeit money 2, false pretences 4, assault and battery 195, disorderly conduct 253, drunk and disorderly 301, vagrants 125, escaped convicts 5, selling lottery tickets 2, conspiracy 2, perjury 1—total number of arrests 1,223."

We speak of this not as a boast, but with shame—but, to correct *evils*, it is necessary to *know* them.

His Honor, Mayor Havemeyer, in his annual message, delivered May 9th of this year, says, while delivering an eulogium on the police :

" From a statement furnished me by the Chief of Police, it appears that from July 8th, 1845, to April 15th, 1848, 67,971 arrests were made ; of which 1,779 were for felonies ; 7,743 for petit larceny ; 42,829 for intoxication and disorderly conduct ; 5,945 for assault and battery ; and 5,175 for vagrancy."

Rather different this, from the times of 1818, according to Cobbett's account.

The correspondent, alluded to above, requests us to account for the increase of crime. To judge from the places of nativity of at least two thirds of the criminals, immigration must be one great cause. All of the large gang of burglars, whom with their real names and characters, we have introduced in our work, are foreigners, mostly Englishmen. The denizens of the horrible circle known as the " Five Points" are principally Irish and negroes ; some few Dutch, are also living there, but not one *American*, to a hundred foreigners, can be found there.

Our Alms Houses are occupied, at the ratio of about fifteen to one, by foreigners, the overflowings of the poor-houses in Europe. The street beggars are principally Irish, Germans, and Italians. When a real American beggar *is* found, he or she is the sauciest, most importunate and insolent of the whole crew—but we may thank our free systems of education, and, above all, our national pride and industry that they are *scarce*.

The immense numbers of emigrants which fill our hospitals and alms-houses, is an evil which bears very heavily upon property-holders and tax-payers in this country, but there seems to be no remedy, although frequent complaints have caused legislative attention to the subject. We have plenty of room in this country for immigrants, if they would seek the unsettled parts; but it is to be regretted that most of the new comers either lack the means or the inclination to go to the interior, and thus become a burden to the inhabitants of the sea-port towns.

But to return to the causes of crime. It is not for the lack of *laws* that crime increases so rapidly, but we are obliged to believe that in a great measure it is owing to laxity in *administering* the laws which have been enacted, and which are neglected by the officers whose duty it is to fulfil them.

We will instance one section of our police law. It says in Section 8 of

AN ACT

To amend an act entitled " An Act for the Establishment and Regulation of the Police of the City of New York." Passed May 7th, 1844.

Passed May 13th, 1846, by a two-third vote.

" It shall be the duty of the Sergeants and Policemen to obey such orders as they may, from time to time, receive from Chief of Police, Captains and Assistant Captains of Police, respecting their duty: and to report through the Captains and Assistant Captains, to the Chief of Police, all violations of the Corporation Ordinances; to preserve the public peace; and it shall be the duty of the Policemen to render every assistance and facility to Ministers and Officers of Justice, and to report to the Captains of their respective Districts, all suspicious persons, all bawdy houses, receiving shops, pawn brokers' shops, junk shops, second-hand dealing shops, gaming houses, and all places where idlers, tipplers, gamblers, and other disorderly and suspicious persons, congregate; to caution strangers and others against going into such places, and against pick-pockets, watch-stuffers, droppers, mock-auctioneers, burners and all other vicious persons; to direct strangers and others the nearest and safest way to their places of destination, and, when necessary, to cause them to be accompanied to their destination by one of the Police, and to perform all other duties which shall be prescribed to them by Ordinance of the Corporation."

Now is it pretended that the policemen, whose stations are in Park Place and that vicinity, know nothing of the large gambling hells kept open there every night? Is it assumed that those who patrol Church, Thomas, Leonard, Duane, Reade, An'hony, and other streets, which are stocked with houses of ill-fame, dance-houses, panel-cribs, thief rendezvous, &c. do not know the whereabouts of these illegal dens, into which strangers are so often ignorantly led, and when there are robbed—and sometimes *murdered!* The present police system, if well carried out, is doubtless the best in the Union, and second to none in the world, except that of London from which it was modelled. Mr. Matsell, the present Chief, is a brave, persevering, energetic man, one who *personally*-attends to more duty than any five of his subordinates--yet we must charge those subordinates who are named in the above quoted section with a gross neglect of their duty, in not making known and arresting the hordes of law-breakers therein mentioned.

If these gambling houses, &c. *cannot* be broken up, if the city government is too weak and sickly to sustain its rights, why not license the gamblers and courtesans, and make the ills which they cannot prevent a source of city revenue.

It is most mortifying to an orderly citizen to see how completely the law is laughed at by criminals—how weak and puny are the efforts of the city authorities to put a stop to immoralities. They made an effort a short time since to put a stop to the "Model Artist" system; to prevent the shameful exhibitions of nude men and women; a few arrests were made —but instead of ceasing, the exhibitors only added to the attractions of their exhibitions, boasting on their show bills of their triumph over law and decency.

While speaking of Model Artists, &c. we are led to remember some very sensible remarks in a letter received from the same correspondent, whose communication we published in our Appendix to No. 3, and though some of his remarks are foreign to this subject, it would mutilate his letter not to give it entire. Therefore we give it all, and the reader will find much information in it, which will lead to comparisons that must be *made* by any close observer, who dwells in the city.

HUDSON, *May* 1, 1848.

DEAR SIR—

I have much satisfaction in perceiving that my communication has been deemed worthy of your consideration. Having been a traveller in my younger days, and contrasting the scenes of public mendicity usual throughout the highways and byways, at the very foot of the crosses or altars in France, as also the tales of practical delusion exemplified in vagrants in the principal streets of Paris or London; *such objects* I confess have not *forcibly struck me* in the city of New York, save in *partial supplication*, or by a *mute appeal*, such as in the extension of the hand, or perhaps more directly by a written petition. Benevolence is a ground which must be cautiously trod upon, on which account men of humanity do not take pains or find leisure to inquire into the correctness of these proceedings.

William Cobbett, like many others, did not add to a strong mind and understanding what is most requisite, *a knowledge of the world*, and was, as you observe in many of his maxims, subject to prejudice. The whole of his life, its aim and tenor, was absorbed in political mania, and I have known persons of the highest commercial consideration, whose fortunes have been ruined, and importance destroyed, from a lack of this qualification. It would require a whole system of legislation to enact an Asylum in which such old babies as Mr. Precise might learn the first rudiments of an education, where the only *true Institution* must be the *world at large*. Now-a-days the young Idea is very precocious, and dreams of matters and things such as have not been heard of by these ancient philosophers. William Cobbett, who was one of the old sect in his times, might have passed 1000 characters of the class he mentions, and still be none the wiser as to what might be their *trade* or *calling*, or be going on at his very elbow. I furnished the extract, not with a view of supporting a similar statement, but for the sake of pointing out to you the impressions of one of the Old School of thirty years ago.

I have heard persons reply to my question, *that they did not admit such volumes (numbers) into their houses, as being of an immoral tendency.* The reasonable grounds for such objections I deny. If they cavil with *due license and expression*, these censures extend themselves to most accounts which involve the peculiarities of our natures, the effects of our passions, and I may include the very body and features of actual life. In this ordeal, the language of Tuscany "raised" in the fourteenth century, would have been lost to the world in the gloom of religious reverie or monastic interference. Petrarch replied to his friend Boccacio, who had been seized with this panic, from the representations of Ciani, a Carthusian Friar, who had been charged with the predictions, and a commission from Father Petronei implying revelations from God affecting his life and writings, "to see Jesus Christ with bodily eyes is indeed a wonderful thing, it only remains *that we know if it be true.*" Judgments in that age might have been formed on *great improbabilities*, as they sometimes now are on very *narrow principles;* and if such were to be the test of merit, no author could outlive his day. Shakspeare in all his visibility and invisibility might have dwindled to an itinerant ballad, monger. And the Bible itself, whose credibility depends so much on its simple narrative, would be shorn of its *impartiality and philosophical details, the very criterion and proof of its genuineness and authenticity*—thus there would be the greatest reason for *complaint* where there is the highest *excellence*.

The knowledge of Letters contributes to promote an accuracy of opinion, and the offspring of humanity is *Life* in all its eventful circumstances. Good lessons are to be learnt even from fiction, but how much the more confessedly, when Literature rests on the stability of truth. In the delineations of Eugene Sue, in his "Mysteries of Paris," incident follows closely, yet faithfully, on incident, murder, blasphemy and all the apathy and weakness of demoniac and fallen nature, with all its dreadful consequences, yet do they say, " this book is a serpent to whisper craftily in the ear of innocence"—*strange indeed the poison, strange and ephemeral. The Boiga unfolding its convolutions in the damps of the dungeon, or hissing melodiously at the foot of the guillotine.*

In the catastrophe the moral, like the penalty, becomes extinct.

When you start a problem it must be solved by drawing conclusions "gradatim;" to support a theory, it behoves you to prove the most practical result. So also to inculcate a moral lesson, you must show forth the consistency of your precepts by a train of argument leading to the actual consequence, or by drawing a parallax from an opposite line of conduct. Short and precise demonstration was the usual Spartan method. Whilst the boys were at their meals their teachers would ask them questions concerning the nature of moral actions, or the different merits of the most noted men of the time, to which they received brief and ready answers, and hence denominated laconic. At other times they would make their slaves drunk, and expose them in that state before children, in order to deter them from this species of debauchery: thus by *opposite* rules they established the forms of discipline and duty. If the Spartan school be justly represented as a model of republican simplicity, who can find fault with the exposure of crime, which has crept into the age in its most dangerous and disgusting features, and designated in your pages?

Perhaps the introduction of the system of Calisthenics in their female exercises, might confound the ideas of the most profound admirers of Spartan economy and government. " They ran, wrestled, pitched the bar, and performed all those feats naked before the whole body of citizens." " Yet this arena," says the historian, " by no means excited a looser appetite." *Our* modern belles are good tacticians, but have no stomach for black broth or a coarser diet; besides a full display in this luxurious age might disturb the frigidity of Lycurgus himself. As the world grew older, it claimed to itself a great share of outward refinement, but much less of primitive and natural virtue; indeed, at last, that quality appear-ed so often under a specious garb, that the true goddess disdaining to wear a mask, blushed to such an extent that many of her votaries and professors scarcely knew her.

We brought up our virgins, cried the Lacedæmonian Sage, in all se-rious severity—in the games the full development of form, limb and muscle, created no evil thoughts or inclinations; for the frequent view of the person curbs sensuality; the Pædonomi, who took charge of our youth, impressed by example—for vice to be abhorred needs only to be seen. Hold, replies our modern Aspasia, our present pattern of virginity would not dare publicly to set eyes on a statue or a naked cupid, but to be admired *they have to be seen*, and as this is the adage they have to make the most of, yet cannot in decency go back to your habits, they do all they can, and what may not naturally be disclosed is left to out-ward ornament, fashion, or what is more valuable, to imagination. Thus connoisseurs of female loveliness charitably impute their very fail-ings to taste and nicety of discernment.

The worthy Burgesses of the upper ten thousand, who have felt their virtue in danger from the "gaucherie" of a petite marchande, Grisette of Division street, or Soubrette of the Cigar Shop, or may not have had op-portunity of detecting original sin in the fairer and higher circles of the daughters of Eve, may now picture to themselves a Paradise, and be-come disciples of the new school of Ethics, and the female Gymnasium on the ancient Lacedæmonian plan in the halls of the Model Artists. Here Venus assumes the attitude by which she gained the palm from her rivals on Mount Ida, or the dishabille in which she was caught with Mars; Juno appears at the bar of the Senate, sueing publicly for a di-vorce, or as "pronuba" presiding over the marriage rites; Lucina giving lectures on Obsteterics; Leander in the state in which he crossed the Hellespont; Atalanta having her run until she has picked up all the golden apples; and, by way of finale, and most pleasing to the manager, Jupiter descends into his mistress' lap in the substance of a shower of gold. All these representations, however grotesque, are not likely to detract from the classic page; the fabulous part may serve to dispense somewhat of attic salt amongst witless clerks and giggling servant girls.

The spectacle at first met with some remonstrance and reprobation. But the Mayor, we are assured, on a certain night (Heaven preserve his Honor and the City from all evil speaking, lying and slandering), peeped clandestinely through a very little hole into this "Camera Obscura," and seeing the *images accompanied by the motions belonging to the objects*, he came to the conclusion that it was a very ingenious piece of mech-anism. On his way home, had not a dark cloud intervened betwixt her and the moon, he might have observed that the figure of justice over aweing the capital was hood-winked and blindfolded, and as the mysterious bandage had not been removed from her eyes, she could not distinguish a Nymph of Anthony street from the Mother of Cupids, and the scales were still hanging, though tottering, in the balance. Motley had been the wear of the Aldermen for some time past, and it was not yet time to change their livery.

No traces have as yet been discovered which can be ascribed to the Odeon of Pericles, and the obliterations of the present age do not unjustly warrant the assertion, that all that remained of this famous specimen of architecture, has been buried in the rubbish that has accumulated on its ruins. Festivals in honor of the Muses have long since ceased: hence it follows, that the bandiness and discrepancies of Pan are mistaken for the chaste attributes and graces of Apollo—but who of our Solons will stoop to judge in this case? Law and decency slumber on the perversion of talent and of taste, whilst every reed of the city, moved by the popular wind, though they do not discern the ears, whispers, " Our Midas is an Ass."

I have read the Metamorphosies of Ovid, seen the " Ombres Chinoises" and Patagonians of the French, have dreamed of imaginary beings, yet, for the life of me, I cannot define how the " beau ideal" is to be personified on earth. Nature, like superstition, fanaticism, and other chimeras, seems to be enveloped in shadow and in doubt, and strange creatures are they that undertake to reveal her mysteries. Must we find the *semblance of the beautiful* in the interesting tableaux and *faultless* forms now under the immediate patronage of the Chief Magistrate and Common Council? there is but one short step from the sublime to the ridiculous: it puts me in mind of an Epigram that appeared many years ago in the Spectator:

> " 'Twixt our Molly and Venus the difference must be,
>   As truly alleged from their birth,
>   For Venus was bred from the *scum* of the sea,
>   Our Molly from *that* of the earth."

Vanity and Folly—life's usual bill of fare—take what is offered with true Epicurean taste, particularly where the viands are served on platters of antiquity—but beware of the fate of Chrysippus, and partake not to excess. You know what happened to that philosopher: he died from *excessive laughter, caused from seeing an Ass eating figs on a silver dish.* silver dish.

I can not, I dare not, as Willis would say, dash at life with a free pencil, but merely catch at a stray beam of reflection that is cast back from the dark side of history.

The Ephesians dedicated temples (εταιρη Αφροδιτη) to the prostitute Venus. Their greatest lawgivers and philosophers held character at a very cheap rate, and supported their opinions both by authority and example.

The temple of Diana, one of the wonders of the world, was bult at the expense of all Asia Minor, but their Goddess was very different from the Virgin and Huntress, and, as described by Montfaucon, was rather the representative of universal nature than of chastity. Athenæus gives a most melancholy account of dissolute practices pervading the whole Grecian system, quoting thus from Demosthenes: "τας μὲν ἑταιρας ἡδονης ἑνεκα ἐχομεν, τας δε παλλακας τῆς καθ 'ἡμεραν παλλακειας, τας δε γυναικας του παιδοποιεισθαι γνησιως, και των ενδον φυλακα πιστην εχειν." "We have courtesans for our pleasure, harlots for daily use, and wives for the legitimate procreation of children, and for the faithful preservation of our property." You know the adage, "Ne cuivis subito contingit adire Corinthum;" or, in other words, you must not venture to Gotham without completing a full insurance. Why attend the modern Artists for a tableau? Lais and Diogenes are daily represented at the steps of each large hotel.

The Gothamites need not turn back to the palmy days of Corinth, or of Ephesus, nor ransack the monuments or luxuries of antiquity. To the Acro-Corinthus overhanging the ancient City, where one thousand courtezans officiated, the crowds extending down slopes diversified with shrines, they can apply in nightly contrast the Promenade of their own Broadway. Domes are not wanting, supported by Corinthian pillars, sufficiently impure for Greek or Roman, Turk or Mahometan; taste and Brass (æs Corinthi) equally splendid, equally spurious; socialism at home, Communism abroad; idols and Idolatry in opposition to the dull Statuary of the ancients; moulds animate or inanimate, to which each modern Prometheus lends his fire to awaken functions of freedom or of life; busts vieing with the marble of Paros, yet like the Sarcophagus containing only the ashes of the noble being which once existed; or where the emblems of pure vitality are not yet extinct, mouldering from the Syrian curse, the leprosy of suspicion. Dianas, like the Mammalia of Ephesus, giving suck to a tribe of bastard imaginations, confounding figures, symbols and mythology. Priests, worthy satellites of their own hells, Pythonesses, Ephesian scrolls and characters (γραμματα εφεσια). What next? Are the whole consequences comprised in the quotation from the Athenian Sage? he merely enumerates the records of public demoralization. The household stock he describes as remaining at home for ordinary purposes, and to increase the breed of sinners, in comparative dependence and security. *In modern Gotham they have other tales to tell.*

And what can we oppose to these growing evils? The cities you speak of, interrupts the churchman, were Pagan, emblems of their times of obscure and darker ages. Yet the early gospel had dawned there: Christianity had been nursed by the apostles, and fostered by general councils. St. Paul had made them the objects of his peculiar solicitude and care. Now Corinth and all its architecture lies in tradition; but few vestiges remain to welcome the eye of the traveller. Her mora.

heathen state was deplorable ; the small light of her regeneration absorbed in her desolation. And of Ephesus, one of those cities whose primitive Church Christ visited in his Revelation, and now blotted from the map.. Mr. Chandler represents the inhabitants as a wretched insensible race, living in the vaults of the Stadium, or the sepulchres which had received the ashes of their Fathers. "We heard," says that intelligent traveller, "the partridge call in the area of the Stadium." Which æra then has humanity mostly to deplore; that of their magnificence and luxury, which led to their degredation, or the very wretchedness of their downfall ? This contemplation diffuses a mournfulness even in' the height of their greatness, whose cadence, like the harp of Morven, revibrates fitfully on the scroll of ages. Yet with what impressions! the moral is the same. Luxury, sooner or later, now as before, produces the same causes, ends in the same effects; like as the serpent that has been represented as the symbol of human passions, it swallows a fertile brood, engendered to its own destruction, and galled by civil or political restraint, "ipsis vinculis sicut fera bestia irritata," like a wild beast gnaws it chains, till it sinks in impotency and prostration.

I have entered thus largely into the fall of these cities, because in your preface, you have dedicated your labors to the clergy, whose efforts in their work have been incessant, yet too often of little effect America has done much abroad through her missionaries, but you are right in your belief, that a much more difficult task remains to the brother laborers in the vineyard, whom they have left at home. The lamp must be supplied, where it needs renovation, and to do these worthy men justice, it does not often happen that the dull flame is allowed to linger in the socket. True Religion is in no wise selfish; it expands itself readily to all who will open their hearts to receive it, and wherever it scatters its seed, it sows in faith and in hope. Like the prairies of the west that rise in importance from the hand of agriculture, so they who have visited *new* lands for the propagation of the gospel, find them in general most *tenacious*—the good fruits are not checked by the weeds and tares, derived from the offals of prejudice or corruption.

Draw a picture from the Rake's Progress, from tales of ordinary life, The drunkard views his face in his glass, and in his altered appearance reads his doom—alarmed as by an apparition, fear lends to him reflection —the memory of former good habits may enact wonders, but fear is the predominant cause of his reform. As with this class, so fares it with all denominations of heretics—to abjure evil propensities requires *strength* of mind, to continue steadfast to good purposes argues the *use* of it. Sin and disease are near akin. As with a thread-worn constitution, so with a thread-worn conscience; the whole tale is comprised in an auld wife's complaint. "Odds rat the old thing, the more you mend, it is still mend, mend, mend, darn, darn, darn, patch, patch, patch, and yet it is ever peeping out at elbows." This is more than a proverb, it is a *fact*. Poverty sensitively confesses it, the rich view it with distrust, and yet the hypocritical world presume to think lightly of it.

Man is of free will and agency, but often gracelessly independent, and jealous in all principles affecting his reason or his science, thus the simplicity and intent of his exemption is arrested in the progress of his refinement, and rather than submit to the harmony of his better nature, it becomes mixed up with the "ignes fatui" of error, speculation and doubt. To this many great minds have been prone, and even to this day the press insists on free tendency of thought and idea, to give scope to pernicious doctrines. When Cadmus sowed the dragons' teeth there arose a host of foes, and these too armed the one against the other, in the full spirit of contention. If man dare not be at direct enmity with his Maker, he becomes inclined to devote it to the destruction of his fellow-creatures. This monstrous birth first engenders scepticism, then an array of evil passions. Against such morbid dispositions has the Christian at home to contend, and most dangerous, as neither amenable to secular power nor law. We hold crime under the statute in abhorrence, because it endangers property, personal safety, the temporal views and well being of society, yet in appeals to self-government and, to self-knowledge, we inherit and hand down to posterity the inherent and indefeasible *right* to enact our own creeds, tenets and opinions.

In this gradation the *public censor* becomes most acceptable; by his practical efforts and knowledge he comes to the aid of the clergy, in scenes with which from the sacredness of their calling, and nature of their avocations they could never have become familiar; if he writes in the spirit of *truth*, the gospel can claim no higher privilege—if these *truths* are daily represented, so may they be daily seen; the gospel has not this immediate advantage; it has to be impressed and explained to be understood.

Put the Mysteries and Miseries in juxtaposition with a religious tract; no matter where—on the mahogany of the rich, on the pine table of the poor; be either of them pious or indifferent, openly or clandestinely, the very character and title of the one, insures a certain degree of reception, and where it is received, its leaves thumb-worn, finger-worn, dogs-eared, denote its use; lend it to a friend, it is a chance if he returns it—the tract would come back with the borrowers best compliments. This is a wayward world to manage. The physician has first to *feel* the pulse, then gild the pill.

Sin is a fascinating minx, yet you have not stopped to ogle with the syren. Spencer, Milton and Marryatt describe her as beautiful in face, but shocking towards the extremities. Some consider that you began at the wrong end; you discarded the lady half, and exposed the monster.

There is a savor of romance in the life of the Missionary, amid

38

savages, or confronting the disciples of Confucius, transforming the Brahmin, Gentoo, South Sea Islander, or native of Southern Africa, and then an isolated being, guided like the shepherds in the wilderness of Bethlehem, and watching the progress of the Star to settle on the home of his pilgrimage and hopes. Next, a spiritual Crusader, midst ruin and desolation flinging aside the ravages and shadows of the past, the antic mockeries of time, and the freaks of the barbarian. Where the mosque has been substituted, or the church confounded in the Moslem, ignorance, superstition, fabulous legends, miracles and relics betokened all that remained of those few denominated christians. These things naturally sprang up from under the tread of the Infidel, blended with the jealousies and traditions resulting from the Patriarchal and Pontifical dissentions. Yet contrast the delusions of these poor unfortunates with Rome, in the 16th Century, with the Bulls and cargoes of indulgences of Leo X. the most sumptuous of Popes. Which system has lent the deepest shades to benight christianity! The ruthless hand of the barbarian, or the mild forbearance of Christ's Vicar on earth!

Cicero's words concerning the presence of a Deity, are most remarkable. "Neque enim gens ulla tam barbara, tam fera, quam non imbuerit Deorum opinio." We see then that the presence and existence constituted an acknowledged and universal rule in heathen philosophy. *Atheism is not the exotic of woods and wilds.* Place such a Professor in a situation apart from the habitations and fermenting discords of his race, where he may have full leisure to devote himself to the study of external nature. In this state he might be led to identify his own life and being, corporeal or intellectual, with what he may discover around him, yet in the objects which meet his attention, the power which he claims to *reason* for himself, denotes the possession of a *distinct faculty which they have not.* It is true that the beasts and brutes of the forest evince sagacity and cunning to assist their properties of strength, and to provide for their wants and safety, but the operations of instinct do not extend to the discernment of right and wrong, weight of causes and effects, power of reflection or government to determine the proper end of human actions. To account for his superiority, he cannot ascribe this extraordinary peculiarity to *chance,* for this would involve the uniform order of things, and the objects he is contemplating contain a general fixed design and character; he must therefore separate the *rational* from the *physical* to make any use of his meditations. But then a difficulty interposes, for to this conclusion he can scarcely arrive, so long as his own nature and bodily *system* is the instrument of the *opposite faculty;* nor can this obedience be imputed to science, for science herself is the offspring of intellect. At this point he has got to the extent of all he knows, or all he can know. He has attempted to dive into the mysticisms of creation, and found no definite satisfaction. He feels and thinks, and yet is perplexed, and thus admits his own dependence and inefficiency ; thus insensible to moral convictions, consistency or responsibilities, his soul reposes on the limits of mortality, partaking of a share of the *essence* yet abjuring the *divine* source from whence it has and derives its being.

Atheism is the garbage of great and powerful cities. A chimera or conceit of the wise opposed to divine perfection. It is singular that it is only found where the word of God is preached. I question much if the missionary finds such a personage in mind and heart, in all his sequestered sojournings or travels.

One word more, and I have done. You have heard the anathema, "oh that my enemy would write a book," and I believe that he who first said so, had all the spirit of malice and uncharitableness in his heart. The life of an author is precarious, full of vicissitudes and disappointments, but I commend you to fame and fortune, and the public morals to the mercies of his Honor the Mayor and Common Council, and all the powers that are or may be. At all events, let me presume to expend a morsel of advice. Try the vein of Democritus. It is always better to laugh than to cry. Ridicule is more powerful than invective. Read Moliére, discard Voltaire. France has now become the theatre of politics and literature. The public will soon feel the fulness of satiety, and the Model Artists commit a moral suicide.

Adieu, L.

We thank our correspondent for his recommendation, and though we do not entirely agree with him in all the points of his letter, we value its general principles, and are indebted to him for the research and historical information which it contains.

But dropping off this part of our work at once, we will here respond to several inquiries which he made in his former letter, and which will be of interest to many of our readers. He says that "It would be a matter of serious consideration, and highly important to your readers, that the *census*, of the city should be introduced, with its several *distinctions, numbers, complexions, houses, grades,*—to ascertain this, even in your spirit of adventure, would be a matter of inquiry from *authority* attended with little difficulty."

Although the matter was a little more difficult than our correspondent seemed to think it would be, we have endeavored to fulfil his and our readers expectations as well as we could.

First, as to population. In 1845, the entire population of the

city, was 371,223 persons, according to Valentine's official city
Manual. Of these, over one third were foreigners. According to
our estimate of increase by immigration, &c. the city population
now cannot consist of less than 425,000 people (probably 450,000),
of whom, nearly one third, *surely* one *fourth*, are foreigners.

We will endeavor to classify some of these people. At the
very least estimate *eighteen thousand* are courtesans, and connected with these, are about five thousand thieves, pocket-book
droppers, burners, watch-stuffers, hack-bucks, mock-auction men,
gamblers, dance-house keepers, grog-shop keepers, pick-pockets,
&c. There are over one thousand *known* houses of ill-fame,
and some of these have from ten to forty inmates. Besides
there are at least one hundred assignation houses, supported by
a more secret and select class of people, who carry vice into
high life.

This is a strange and a hard story to tell of the great Me-
tropolis of the Union, but there is more *truth* than poetry in it.
Church street alone, from Chambers to Canal street, contains
near fifteen hundred women of ill-fame, with whom are connected the other characters alluded to above.

There are only 225 churches in New York, to contrast with
the above, the average Sabbath attendance at *altogether*, as
near as we can judge, being only about 60,000, less than one
seventh, and with these counting in all the children who attend
sabbath schools, &c.

We have not been able to get the number of liquor-shops,
but judging from calculations formed by counting the numbers
in several districts, they cannot be *less* than two thousand. Of
these about fourteen hundred are low holes, where an adulter-
ated poison called *gin* is principally kept, and which is not
quite as quick but fully as sure to produce death as prussic acid.

In the population of the city there are now supposed to be
about 16,000 blacks. They have ten or twelve separate churches.

We have, in several places in our work, animadverted rather
severely upon the inefficiency of our city government, but we
have now reason to believe that the new Mayor, Hon. W. F.
Havemeyer, is about to institute a new order of affairs.

On the 20th of May, two of the leading gamblers in town,

one of them a *character* in the " Mysteries," were arraigned and *fined*; we see that an establishment in Reade street, which we named in a letter addressed to his Honor, on the 1st of May, has also been broken up. These things look promising, and if the Mayor will only follow the business up and *fine* the keepers of gambling hells upon every occasion of detection, he will not only add materially to the city revenue, but also do himself and his city a lasting benefit. If we do not err, during his first administration, he was the first to use steps toward breaking up the business of the rascally Peter Funk, or mock-auction men, and he has yet a large field of these kind of weeds to set his policemen to work in.

We have no political prejudices, and belong to no party, but will at all times give all the little influence which we may possess, toward supporting and retaining those men in office who will firmly, honestly, and fearlessly do their duty, regardless alike of interest, threats or bribes. We detest cowardice anywhere—but in office particularly.

In our letter alluded to above, addressed to his Honor the Mayor on the 1st of May, and to which we received a kind response, we estimated that the gamblers of all classes, black and white, not including " policy dealers," amounted to *three thousand.* We said that if these persons were arrested and *fined* according to *law*, the city would gain *seven hundred and fifty thousand dollars* by the operation; and that if only five hundred of them were thus dealt with, the snug sum of *one hundred and twenty-five thousand dollars* would be raised, which would much lessen the burden of our many tax payers, and there are at *least* five hundred gamblers employed at their villainous trade, each night, within ten minutes walk of the Mayor's office.

If it should be found impossible to break them up by *fining*, we certainly could apply some of their ill-gotten gains to good purposes; for instance, to establish a home for the families of those whom they have ruined, which families are frequently left in destitution and want. It would be better at once to *license* them, than to permit them to go on with their systems of robbery in open *defiance* of the law. We do not think however that it would be very difficult to break up this gang of criminals, especially at this time—for by long neglect they have been lulled into a security which makes them perfectly careless. A policeman, or any body else, can walk into 3 Park Place, 14 Barclay street, and other "Hells" in that neighborhood, any evening, and see the "game" carried on, "without fear and above board."

There are thousands of dollars won, we might say *stolen*, in those places every night—why shouldn't the city treasury have a share of it? If we cannot do away with an evil, let us do the best we can with it.

Mr. Pat Hearn and Mr. Berry each paid in a $100 *contribution* on the 20th May, why not cause the rest of the "fraternity" to "walk up to the captain's office" and do likewise.

Colton, Suydam, Harrison, and a hundred or two more of their "particular and aristocratic set" can afford a C. full as well as Hearn and *Berry*. The latter, of all in town belonging to his profession, is the most honorable and best principled, for he has been known to give back money won at his "bank," when he found that it was lost by a *minor*, and that it belonged to a widowed mother. We are not aware that any other member of "the brotherhood" has been guilty of a similar action.

But we will leave these gentry to the care of His Honor, and look at some other *miseries*.

THE POOR.—By the Alms House report, we learn that the city supports in the Alms House, Hospitals, &c., 5368 people. A class of out-door poor relieved every two weeks, amounts to about 2300. 12,200 applications for *fuel* have been made in the past year.

Besides, there are a vast number of persons who are too proud to apply for relief, who suffer far more than many who are in the above enumerated. From the Tribune of March 17th, we extract the following account of a Society, which we most particularly recommend to our city readers.

"THE SUFFERING POOR.—We extract the following items from the monthly report of the 'Association for Improving the Condition of the Poor,' believing they will be as gratifying to others as they have been to ourselves. It will be recollected that this extensive and efficient charity employs 300 gentlemen visiters, whose services are gratuitous, and who always visit the poor at their homes before granting relief.

During the past four weeks the number of families relieved was, - - - - - - 3,693
Number of persons relieved, - - - - 13,475
Number of visits, - - - - - 6,206
Expenditure, - - - - - $5,160 10

"The two most striking of the above facts are the *economy* of the expenditure and the vast amount of *gratuitous service.* Though more than 6,000 visits of sympathy, counsel and aid have been made to the abodes of the indigent within a month, we are assured that the statement falls far short of the actual attention and labor bestowed by the devoted visitors. For their visits being both for investigation and relief, each often requires numerous calls of inquiry on different families, that the true character of the applicant may be known before aided. Surely their self-denying, philanthropic labors, operating irrespective of every sectarian or national distinction, should be liberally sustained. We regret, however, to learn, that the Association is greatly straitened for funds. Many supposing the mildness of the winter had diminished the wants of the Poor, have given less liberally, or altogether withheld their contributions. This is a great mistake. The extensive prevalence of sickness, desertion of families by enlistments in the army, and the unusual number of destitute immigrants, are among the causes peculiar to the season which more than counterbalance any trifling advantages of weather, and have produced more suffering and want than have been known for many years. Who, knowing these facts, will not double their contributions, or, according to their ability, lend a helping hand to save their fellow-creatures from suffering and death? Send your checks without delay to R. B. Minturn, Treasurer, 78 South-st."

And we have also a large and regularly systematised band of street beggars, who "go in for making money," many of them being employed by persons already wealthy, whose riches have been amassed in this way. Women go about with borrowed or stolen children—men who never were beyond the precincts of a town, apply for aid in consequence of " wounds received in the wars," &c. But it is easy to detect these impostors, and *charity,* the brightest of all human virtues, need never be thrown away.

Many complaints are made as to the manner of distributing

the city charities. And we also find that many of the so called charitable Societies and Asylums, are rather speculating associations than anything else. For instance, we find the following occurrences before the Board of Supervisors, on the 16th of April.

"BOARD OF SUPERVISORS.—*Lunatic Asylum.*—The principal subject acted upon was the petition of the institution to be relieved from about $200 tax, being the rate on 640 lots ground, owned by it, contiguous to the Asylum. A debate arose on the propriety of doing so, some of the members taking the ground that it was a charity and entitled to exemption from tax, while others held the reverse. It was stated that the Asylum keeps purchasing property which pays tax, and then claims that it is exempt from such. As a proof that it is not a charity it was said that it refused to receive, unless paid for, the widow of an Alderman [Ald. Smith we believe of the Fourth Ward] who perished during the cholera of 1832; his wife became insane and remained so for several years at Blackwell's Island, and finally died. It was also said, by Ald. Purser, that the Asylum keeps the *airy, good rooms, in the centre of the building exclusively for those who can pay $10, $8 and $5 a week, while those who pay but $3 a week have to occupy the wings, and are not so well off as the insane patients at the Alms-House Hospital.* He considered that the donation of $22,500 given by the State to the Asylum would be much more appropriately employed if given for the general use of the City Hospital, of which the Asylum is said to be a branch. The resolution in favor of remitting the tax *was adopted:* 11 to 5!! Ald. P. then offered a resolution to the effect, that the Board, while exempting the Asylum from tax, *regrets that the funds of the State are not equally applied among the several inmates.* Ald. McElrath, and other members, thought if there was really cause of complaint the proper way would be to appoint a committee to confer with the Governors of the Hospital, or in some other way to ascertain it. The resolution, for the present was laid upon the table."

Here we find an Association, pretending to be a *charitable* one, which makes distinctions in its inmates according to their ability to pay, and then after having received a donation of $22,500, from the state, asking to be freed from paying taxes upon *only* SIX HUNDRED AND FORTY !!! lots of fast improving property. The heirs of Astor ought also to apply to have their taxes remitted. The petitioners certainly live at the Asylum, and those who voted for the remission deserve a place in it.

While speaking of insanity, we are reminded of the report of the N. Y. State Asylum. Among the many causes for insanity recorded, we find the following:

Religious anxiety, 152—76 males and 76 females.
Intemperance, 50—47 males and 3 females.
Millerism, 33—14 males and 19 females.
Disappointment in love, 39—23 males and 16 females.
Perplexity of business, 41—28 males and 13 females.
Abuse of husbands, 24—females.
Excessive labor, 15—10 males and 5 females.
Political excitement, 6 men.
Disappointed ambition, 7—5 males and 2 females.
Excessive pain, 4 men.
Seduction, 3 females.
Remorse, 3 men.
Study of Phrenology, 1 male.
Anticipation of wealth, 3—1 male and 2 females.
Excitement of law suit, 1 female.
Ill-treatment of parents, 2—1 male and 1 female.
Anti-Rent excitement, 1 male.

There are also several private Insane Asylums, near the city which are generally well filled; and one at Flushing, L. I., under the charge of Dr. James M'Donald, a very humane and excellent man, is spoken very highly of.

New York is by no means destitute of societies which are charitable in name and intent, but the systems of many of these are so imperfect that they do very little good. For instance, few, very few reformations occur in the Magdalen Asylum, because the unhappy inmates who fly there to forget their errors, and to reform, are continually reminded of them. The dark past, instead of being buried in oblivion, as it should be, is kept ever present before them.

Upon asking a wretched creature who had endeavored to reform, and who had been an inmate of this Institution, why she had returned to her sickening life, she replied:

" They did nothing but preach up to me what I had been, until they almost made me sick of life !"

Had this poor creature been led kindly on, no allusions made to the past, but a bright and virtuous future kept before her, there is no doubt but that she would have been reformed.

There are between thirty and forty Societies here, which can properly be termed "Benevolent Associations." Among them we can name,

The "New York Hospital," which was founded in 1771, by the Earl of Dinmore; the "Bloomingdale Insane Asylum" (which is getting rich, and of course less charitable); "Lying in Hospital" for destitute females (an excellent and praiseworthy institution); "Marine Society," "Mariner's Industrial Society," for furnishing employment to the female members of seamen's families, and aiding such as are in distress, or are incapable of labor (an institution which cannot be too highly praised); "The American Shipwreck Society;" "British and Irish Protective Emigrant Societies;" "Welsh Benevolent Society;" "New York Dispensary;" "Northern and Eastern Dispensaries;" "Deaf and Dumb Institute;" "Institution for the Blind;" "Asylum for aged and *Respectable* females," into which we understand there is very great difficulty of admission, in consequence of the different standards by which respectability is judged; "Magdalen Asylum;" "N. Y. Orphan Asylum;" "Leake and Watt," ditto; "Roman Catholic" ditto; two "Colored" ditto; "Prison Association," one of the noblest of all charities; "St. George," "St. Andrew," "St. David," and, last but not least, the ancient and honorable "St. Nicholas Society."

There are others which we have not named, which perhaps in their quiet way, do full as much good as the most prominent and showy.

If all of these associations were conducted upon a broad, free-handed system of *true* charity; kept open to the really poor, and managed by persons who study human nature in their efforts to do good, how much suffering they would alleviate. There is money enough *given* yearly in New York, to place all its poor in comfort, if it were judiciously applied. Those who are able and willing to give, should be careful to bestow their charities upon those who really need it, and avoid giving funds to aid in the foolish theories and experiments which some of the societies are always trying. The out-door Association, so far as we can judge from observation of its activity and effects, seems to us to be one of the most deserving. We allude to that mentioned on a former page, of which Mr Minturn is Treasurer. We approve of this, because it employs *visitors*, who first *see* the applicants for aid, and learn whether they indeed need it or not, before they give it. No impostor can steal charity from them, to the loss and detriment of the really needy. During the past winter they have done much good. Many of our readers will scarcely believe that in this great city, where so much wealth is lying idle, and where so many people live in careless ease and luxury, persons have *died* from cold, exposure and want during the past season. Yet it is true. And many of our readers will scarcely believe that there is so much crime here as we have described. They will think that our "old Brewery" scenes, &c. are overwrought. We will not only refer them back to Mr. Matsell's certificate, but ask them to read the following item from the "*National Police Gazette*" of May 13th, a paper which is always *independent and bold*, and which contains more police information, and more *statistics* of crime, than all the rest of the papers in the Union, put together. The extract is as follows.

"MYSTERIOUS MURDER.—Most of the readers of this paper have heard of the Old Brewery, on the Five Points in this city, a place where it is supposed many deeds have been committed that will never be developed in this world. On Friday night a party of scavengers commenced operations for cleaning out the sink of this building, and on removing the floor thereof, they discovered the body of a man in an advanced stage of decomposition. With the aid of the police the body was removed to an adjoining apartment, where it appeared to be almost impossible for the remains ever to be recognized: but there is enough to presume that they are those of some unfortunate man who had been decoyed there, or had involuntarily strayed into that den of infamy, and was robbed and murdered. The situation in which the body was found, with the size of the aperture, precludes the possibility of any man having fallen in the sink by accident.—Another fact is the dress, which, so far as can be judged, appears to have been of the best materials and of fashionable make. The teeth are in good preservation—very white and regular. A black silk handkerchief was round the neck, from which fact, it is presumed the unfortunate man was **not** one of the habitues of the Five Points. An inquest was held yesterday by the coroner, but nothing could be ascertained as to the mystery."

If some of our disbelieving readers would take a night-stroll down into that sickening neighborhood, and look around amongst the wretches who hide away during the day, and come out at night, half-naked, reeking with filth and gin-fumes, they would think them fit for any crime which the devil could invent, and man perpetrate.

The above is not a solitary item hunted up to sustain our positions, but one only of hundreds. There is not a day that the coroner does not hold inquests upon persons "found dead," sometimes in the water, sometimes on land. Do all of these die a natural death—are all of them "*accidentally*" drowned? No, indeed. We fear that many a man thus found has been drugged in the thieving cribs, robbed and then cast into the water to save further trouble. Of course we cannot unravel these "mysteries;" but from the many cases, and the facts connected with them, we are forced into this belief.

It would be a blessing to New York, if every one of the horrible dens which form the neighborhood call the "Five Points," was burned to the ground. Until such an event does take place, it will be as it now is, a nest for thieves and murderers. The dark and narrow alleys, deep cellars, houses with secret communications from street to street, &c. afford safe places for concealment and escape to all criminals, and when once a thief gets fairly into that region, if the whole police of the city are after him, he will get away. No one can form an idea of this place, unless they visit it, and then they must not merely pass along the main streets, but they must dive into the dark holes and alleys, and see things as they are "behind the scenes," as the writer of this work has in many a dark and sickening hour, at night, when he was employed in gathering materials for this and forthcoming books.

While speaking of this, we are reminded of a letter received some time since, from a very singular and original correspondent, who says that we "know nothing of New York," though we have been preparing for this work *only* two years, the last of which has been spent in active researches.

The *original* of the letter which we here subjoin, and which we publish *exactly as it is written*, using the original spelling punctuation, &c. can be seen by the curious, for a short time, at our publishing office, 2 Astor House, but as Barnum has made us an offer for it, through one of his agents, the curious must call early to see it. The poor can have a sight *gratis;* all others, if they *say* they are respectable, can do likewise.

"*NED BUNTLINE,*"
Care of *Berford & Co.*,
No. 2 *Astor House.*

To—
Ned   *New York City*
Honored Sir
Saturday 2 o'clock P M

Greatly do I congratulate you—for the path you are now delving as it regards the "Western Queen of Cities."

Yet with strict purity of principle, and wisdom of conclusion I am oblige to say—all in all that you as an individual knows but little of *New York City.*

But my object in adressing your personage, at this Junction— standing as I profess to do before the Altar of my Divine Master with a character—free from terpitude or reproach—from that craveing plight of sinful amusement—such as 20,000 Mortals are trafficking in by day and by night—and one free from the beaten paths of Gamblers, stands him who now address your personage.

Yet after all this—blessed with eyes and ears, I have a perfect right valid and impartial, to see—hear and behold whatsoever things I do wittsness and plunge into for the millions— scenes which should be heraleded to the wide spread world throughout earths remotist bounds.

For the last 8 months I have from time to time portrayed on paper things which at some future day I thought I should lay before the Public—Mysteries of this City—Just—impartial and accurate.

Yes—strange things I could tell of this New York City—yet since your work has come out—the question is often asked "Why dont Buntline come out and portray to light some of our fashionable houses Why talk eternally bout "Big Lize" and so on."

Certainly, sir this should be done and He who rules and guides his thrones upon the ruling spheres would uphold you in so doing. But to add to my Writings I have taken the unfeigned pains—contriving plans in the Future that I might obtain what I have by my own eyes and mouth.

Now as it would add greatly to your work and nothing indecorous in the least degree—I stand ready to grant to you this —to portray to you on paper each in separate chapters—of 12 the very first fashionable Houses of Ill-fame—the street the number and some there are in Broadway—display richly the furniture—costly paintings heavy drapery—divans, satin cushions chandeliers—ottomans—huge mirrors—the Girls names— how many in numbers—where some sprung from—the woman who keeps the house, the manner a girls dressed—the Gamblers who visit—doctors—clerks—elite—&c &c.

Saying nothing but what I should be willing—before a Magistrate to take a solemn oath.

All this from these Houses myself by plans have obtained, and then sanctioned by many chamber maids whom I have caused by presents to tell me confidentially their names. Enter Squire Buntline if you choose 55 or 50 Leonard Street—inspect *all things human* and of pampered Art within those walls—and how quickly you will say that no other house is better furnished than such.

Sir I could add unbounded Joy to your comeing volumes and I will do this—all I ask is a small compensation enough to pay for time—the price left solely to you—and will do it. Please leave an answer with Berford & Co. or address Post Office at early date.   Yours, &c.

                                                H. G. BRADY.

We do not know whether this is our "eagle-eyed" correspondent's "*real* name" but we'll bet a "lump of gold" that his information is worth considerably less than one cent, and that he had better do up a book on his own account, and run an opposition with us. Of course we gave the gentleman a polite rejection of his very kind offer.

We know nothing of New York? Where is the certificate which we publish on our covers, from *the* man of *all* men who knows "New York as it is?"

Let the reader peruse the following letter, which can also be seen at our publishers, from a good man, who *is* known, and not only gives his *real* name, but mentions his high and holy calling, and gives points which prove him to be no imposter.

Brownsville, Pa. May, 22, 1848.

MR. JUDSON,
  Dear Sir:

I have read with lively interest Nos. 1, 2, 3, 4 of the "Mysteries and Miseries of New York," and truly they have brought to my mind many scenes that I have witnessed in the city in the line of my profession, that is, " Marriages."

I resided in New York six years, from May 1834 till May 1840, during which time I married upwards of nine hundred couples. And you no doubt can call to recollection my name, that you have often seen under the head of marriage notices. I preached at the corner of Norfolk and Broome streets.

I was often called upon, under the most mysterious circumstances, to solemnize marriages. Sometimes I would be taken in a closed hack to places, and the most strict secresy enjoined. And these places I never could find afterwards. Other times, persons would come to my house, 69 Pitt street, where I then lived, at late hours, in closed carriages, with the same secresy enjoined, for reasons they then gave, of rich uncles or aunts who would disinherit them if they should find it out. I could furnish you with several instances if you should ever desire them, that you could do well with in writing some other publication. I will furnish them if you wish.

I wish to read No. 5 of the " Mysteries," and have written to your publishers to forward it to this place; please do not let them neglect it.

Yours, Respectfully,
MR. JUDSON.*   ISAAC N. WALTER.

Our book was dedicated to the clergy, and we have to thank them generally, both in this city, Brooklyn, and all over the Union, for a most liberal and cheering patronage and encouragement.

Knowing as they have, that our work had *truth* for its foundation, and moral reform for its aim, they have alluded to it in the most liberal and friendly terms, from their pulpits, and have satisfied us that we have at least partially succeeded in our object of doing good.

* Any information which our reverend and esteemed correspondent will send **us** will be thankfully received, and *used*.

A friend from Kentucky—one of the most influential men in Logan County, and a member of a church there, says, that the work is there sought after by every one—and read by persons who never before took a novel in hand.

Here is another letter from an anonymous correspondent, who seems to think that we know very little of New York. The *original* of all letters which we publish, can always be seen at our office. We do not of course publish all which we receive—some of them are entirely too complimentary (over the left), others rather too illegible, as if written by nervous hands. By the way, speaking of this, will our anonymous correspondents do us the favor to pay the postage. We are, it is true, doing very well with our book, but we had rather not pay away money upon a mass of useless literature—letters which we cannot use, and which can not even make us angry. If you'll write them saucy enough to stir up our ebeneezer, and make us feel lively, we'll pay postage with pleasure—but we are decidedly averse to the mamby pamby trash which we get loaded in upon our table through the post.

But to this letter. Here it is.

Mr. Edward Z. C. Judson
Author of the
" *Mysteries & Miseries of New York.*"
City of New York.

Sir—
A few days since your " Mysteries of N. Y." fell into my hands, I have read them with pleasure, but I am suprised, and sorry to learn that you have announced your intention of publishing but one number more, viz. No. 5. It seems to me that the work ought to be continued, for there is certainly a sufficiency of matter to be found to fill many numbers more. You perhaps are not aware to what extent the whole country is overrun with hordes of " *Gamblers, Swindlers, Robbers,* " libertines" *Murderers* seducers, &c. (many of whom are dressed like Gentlemen,) and are traveling on, The Rail Roads, Steamboats, &c. &c. and who are connected with their associates, in the Cities, and act in concert throughout the land, are organized into regular *Bands,* some giving information, and assisting one another as the case may require.

The greatest proportion of crimes are undoubtedly committed, in the cities, for the reason that large Cities are more favorable for concealment than in the country, and that more persons having money are concentrated, in the City, on business, *requiring money*, and who are watched, and followed from the Country and the City. Where there are members of the *Gang*, engaged in some of the largest Hotels of the Cities, some engaged in the capacity of Clerks, Chambermaids, Porters, Servants, &c. &c. and when an individual who is known to have or supposed to have money comes into the city, and who is alone, and appears to be what they call "Green," he is at this hotel taken to a room on an upper floor, and is told that as soon as a vacancy occurs, (which is expected in the course of the day) he shall be accommodated with a more convenient room but no room is seldom found vacant for him on the first day. In the course of the first night the door of the new lodger is opened with false keys, and if the occupant should be asleep, he is only robbed of his money, and left to finish his sleep undisturbed, but should he awake and attempt to give an alarm he is silenced, and perhaps put out of the way where his body will never be found. It would appear incredible to many who have not had experience, but such are the facts. I have heard many make remarks with regard to *your* publications, and say that they do not believe the reality, or believe that *your* statements are founded on facts. For myself I believe that you have not exaggerated. Indeed I do not think that you are yourself aware of one half or even one tenth part of the Crimes that are committed throughout the land, or City.

Have you ever Read, or heard an account of a desperate "Gang," in C. W. called the "*Markham* Gang"! so called, from the circumstance, of the Gang having fixed its head quarters at a towhship called Markham, situated a few leagues from Toronto. (Canada West.)

The Markham Gang was Partially Broken up, one, or two years ago, by the vigilance of a worthy, and active Magistrate of the City of Toronto—several of the Gang were arrested, tried and convicted and sent to the State Prison, others made their escape.

The worthy magistrate who was so instrumental in ferriting out and bringing the markham vilains to Justice, cautions the Public to be on their guard. For *he*, says that he has discovered that a ramification of the "*Markham* Gang" extend throughout the Provinces of Canada, and also throughout the U. States, and are linked together. A discription of the "Markham gang" was given some two years ago, and Published in a Newspaper

39

of the City of Toronto—called, The *"British Colonist."* If you have never read, or heard a discription of the so called " Markham Gang," you can obtain ample information by applying to any of the Magistrates of Toronto (Canada West) and I really hope that you will take the trouble to do it—You have undoubtedly entered into the subject with no other than honest and worthy motives and I heartily wish you success, and hope you will push on your investigations, and publications, until you have made the whole of the community open their eyes, and see the danger to which they are exposed, if this lawless, and desperate gang of *desperadoes* is not *watched,* ferreted out, and brot to justice. Were I more favorably situated, I would enter into the cause, and at all hazards, and perils, use all my feeble powers, towards breaking up, and *Breaking Down* " and destroying, *root and branch,* that *abominable,* and *Desperate,"* Gang of *Robbers, Thieves, Libertines,* " *Gamblers, Swindlers,* &c." which is becoming stronger and more powerful, *every year,* every month and every day.

What I have here stated is not imaginary, but is what I positively know to be, *truth.*

• I hope you will pardon the liberty I have taken in writing this hasty, very *unconnected,* Epistle—and addressing it to you.

I shall not put my name to it for the reason that I do not know how it may be received by you but I hope that you will receive it favorably, and besides I do not think my signature or name could be of any benefit to the cause and I do not wish to have my name called in question, all I can now say I am sincerely a friend to the cause you have undertaken.

I have the honor

      Sir

      To assure you that I am sincerely your friend and your most Obedient, and most humble Servant

      A. B. C.

N. B.—Should you change your mind, and conclude to continue your publications and you should desire it, I will communicate to you my name Residence &c. &c. and the sources whence my information is obtained give you all the information in my possession, and however should you desire to know the author of this, hasty, written epistle, written without method, or order, and almost illegible hand, you will Please to address a line To A. B. C. and drop it into the Post Office."

[We give letters, exactly as they are written and punctuated.]

We thank our unknown correspondent for the trouble he has taken and the information which he has given. If he will call upon us, we will be glad to confer with him, and see what we can learn of the matters to which he alludes.

We are not averse to receiving *correct* information from any reliable source, if it is not offered through motives of *personal* malice toward those who are accused.

Persons have frequently volunteered information against others, in "high life," &c. but in so many cases we have found out that personal *enmity* was their chief inducement, that we are very careful who we listen to, or what evidences we receive. There are so many people who have slander worked into their very nature; who are prejudiced against everything and everybody but their own self-loved selves; and who seem to enjoy detraction as they do food and drink, that a writer cannot be too careful to whom he listens when preparing a work like this. In taking this firm and independent course we are sure to make foes of those whom we will not oblige by becoming their tools of revenge—and of course place our name in their lying mouths, that they may vent their spleen at us before every grog-shop caucus—but their condemnation is the *praise* which we most covet.

Somebody, Shakspeare we believe, says that "a villain's slander is an honest man's praise." We, then, should be obliged to sundry *bar-room orators*, and "rough-draft" letter writers, who read to others communications to us, abusing us, which we never receive—for the *praise* they give us.

The general reader will of course take this to be an allusion to some particular person, or persons. It *is*, and is intended as a well-merited rebuke to a person whom we cannot well reach in any other way, though if we chose to make him amenable to law, we could have the pleasure of seeing him placed either in an Insane Asylum, or a prison, for sundry threats against our life, &c. But as we have not the slightest idea that the person alluded to, ever meant to, or would dare to put his threats into execution, we have concluded to "laugh at him and let him slide." We do not mention names—because we only wish *the* individual, and such persons, as having listened to his orations, will readily recognize him, to know what we think of the matter. N. S. on that point.

At this moment while finishing up this friendly gossip with the readers who have followed us through our story, we have had our attention called to a pamphlet lately issued in this city, and which we believe comes under the character of works prohibited by law as "licentious and obscene," which work, however, alludes to us in various places, *attempting* to praise us. As this work in its style very much resembles the letter which we publish on page 109, we presume that the writer of it has determined to *do* a book on his account. If he has, it is a decided and unmitigated *do*.

As an item of information in his work is quite important, we copy it for the purpose of making an inquiry. He says:

"Selden & Carlton, Meadows & Livingston, Lawrence & Co. threaten to *ring* Ned Buntline's nose—and for what? Because he has performed one pious, honest act—he has told the *truth:* because, like the Good Samaritan, he has poured "oil and wine into their bruises;" judged righteous judgment, and scaled the walls of their corruptions and iniquity."

The question we have to ask is—if these gentlemen are going to *ring* our nose, what kind of metal will they use? Judging from the style and language of the writer from whom we quote, *he* has monopolized all the *brass* in the country, perhaps with a wish of speculating.

This writer thanks us for telling the truth, yet in his preface he charges our work with being a *pretension*, while he claims for his work alone, the *truth*, and modestly says he has "Wisdom and Truth to guide and govern *his* conclusions, aided by a strict propriety of language and purity of principle, &c."

We, of course, cannot *say* so, but we cannot help thinking that this is the same person who wrote to us, offering, for "a small compensation,"* a good deal of information, which would have been like a farm we know of out West. There is a great deal of rock on it—but unfortunately no soil, therefore it is *unproductive.* He seems to have been offended at our refusal of

---

* As the work is not sold in respectable book stores, we expect that the writer will fulfil his desires in regard to the "small compensation."

his offer. He speaks of his work of exposing the doings of people in high-life. Judging from his grammar and orthography, of which last we have just given a specimen, his knowledge of high-life, must be rather limited. His style is certainly *very* original.

But we have a little more to say about this person, taking the same liberty with him that he has with us. He says, that

"With a character free from stain or reproach, he humbly trusts he stands clad in 'mail and armor of proof' impregnable and secure. To all distrustful minds he would say—'Be vigilant to catch the bear before you sell his skin.'"

We have all heard of the old fable about the "Ass in the Lion's Skin," but what kind of an animal is under this "bear-skin" we cannot imagine. It cannot be an Ass, for that animal though stupid, is honest and useful, and through the extra exertions of the "John Donkey," a universally read and very witty Philadelphia paper, is becoming quite famous. We hope that the bear-skin do'n't cover what a great many *bare* skins do, not "a *lump* of gold," but of humbuggery and corruption.

We are glad to learn from the author's repeated assurances in various parts of his pamphlet, that his character is "free from stain or reproach," but we acknowledge that we cannot be convinced that he has written entirely for "*public good ;*" we cannot from appearances feel certain of his boasted honesty and "purity of principle." Yet he preaches well. Hear him:

"Dare any one harbor the unjust thought, that in these Legends, falsehood, fraud and corruption shall be sold in the market to the highest bidder?"

We reckon, calculate, guess, assume and judge, yes, Sir-ee!

This person, whatever his *real* name may be, has written several letters, the originals of which are now in the hands of the proper authorities, threatening these persons, that if they did not *pay* him for *not* doing it, he would "show them up." The thought is very "*unjust,*" is it not, and it would be still more unjust to think that a foreigner of no particular extraction, who left his country for reasons best known to himself, and came to this "Western Queen of Cities," should be too lazy to work, too timid to steal, and should take to lying as the easiest mode of getting a living. If this person had really undertaken his labors with an honest desire to do good, if he did not try to sell out to the "highest bidder," he would have found in us, not an opposer, but a friend.

There is a broad field here for laborers—we are not fearful of rivals, or tender of competition, but we like to pull in a team of blood horses ; we don't wish to see a nondescript animal come alongside of us, and profess to be that which he is not. There is vice enough in the city to employ many people in rooting it out, but we wish no "devil upon two sticks," to take a stand amongst the laborers—one who has learned the "games" he "pretends to describe," by peeping in through window-blinds, and corrupting chambermaids, as he says. But hear *him* say how he got his information :

"The author, in writing these Legends, places nothing before you gathered from doubtful sources, or from the pen or lips of policemen ; but all that is told you he has witnessed and seen, by day and by night, with his own *eagle eye*.

"Say not—nay, let no thought or dark conjecture enter your heart, that he who depicts, in truthful colors, deeds and scenes which the actors therein deemed safely locked within their own bosoms, is himself a trafficker in these sinful pleasures."

Of course not—*we* would not accuse him of anything of the kind, though from the repeated assurances of his innocence given throughout his work, one is led to imagine that he very much fears of being suspected as a "*trafficker*," &c., &c.

But we must here quietly convict him of a small slip of the pen, which the uncharitable may possibly term a falsehood— or rather a tissue of them.

After describing a scene, which may or may not be true, he closes up his remarks, thus :

"Numerous circumstances of a similar character have been *told* us, as have been enacted under this 'form and manner.' We have, also, had the fact portrayed to us by an M. P."

"M. P." is meant to stand for "Municipal Police," here ; yet in the quotation above, this person with his "pen—veracious and fearless," says that nothing in his work has been gathered from policemen. In various other places he gives information which he says he *has* received from others ; and by *one* in particular, " Black Joe," he has been most egregiously " stuffed."

Hear how the *saint* goes on—let " the millions" pause and listen to his bray !

" Before the millions, we speak TRUTH ! Our cause is just, our course bold and fearless, and so far as we have the faculty of speech, our language shall be clear, to the point, and such as all may read without hesitation—and reading understand.

" Shall we fatigue and tax the brain with scenes which have occurred around and within the ' Hook ?' Shall we indulge, time after time, in scouring the precints of the far-famed and classic ' Five Points,' and describing by the score the acts and dealings, the insinuations and debaucheries of ' Big Lize,' and those low dens of infamy ? Or do you earnestly wish that, to the doings of the *elite*—of what is called to-day the ' fashonable circles'—we should turn our eye ?

" Listen, and we will speak our purpose.

" In these LEGENDS we shall write of none save the first fashionable houses of ill-fame—those conducted in the most costly and luxurious style, both in manner and form, and frequented by persons of the highest stand and most unsuspected characters. To *others* we leave a description of the common bagnois and the degraded inmates who inhabit them. Ours is a higher mark !

Little are the thousands aware that houses of high degree and of fashionable resort—which will be designated and called by name in these Legends—are situated within the most brilliant thoroughfares of this city, hardly known save by those who own or control them, and the ' choice spirits' who visit them.

" Courteous reader, let us assure thee, that in the ' ower true tales' that we shall tell, the scales of impartial justice shall be touched by an even, though a cautious, calm, and *downy* hand."

Let us see how these " scales of impartial justice," would be turned by a " lump of gold," in that *downy* hand.

Read the following letters, if you please, and see how very incorruptible this *pious* man is. The originals are in the hands of the civil authorities at this time, and the " bear" would be too, if he could be found. But he is stowed away in his " *den*," and those who want the "skin" can't catch the animal. He is a great boaster, and if his "*honesty*" is not all assumed why does he hide himself from the public?

We have received permission to copy the two letters which are below, from the city authorities, in whose hands these and many others of a similar kind have been placed, in order to bring the writer to justice if he or his pretended publishers can be found. They are literally as follows—the names only being left blank.

The reader will here observe how *honest* this saint is, and also note how well educated this associate of the *elite* is, for we copy every word and line verbatim.

To   Friday Eve,
    Mrs
        ___ ___ ___   *Astor Place*
                        Dear Madam,
By this period of time—doubtless you have perused with an eagle eye—my Work—styled "Asmodeus or Legends of New York"—which great and impartial work of months—toil—time—money and variance of life, will be completed in 10 sepperate volumes—each book of 100 pages—making entire 1000 pages.

I have in a feeble manner, as a minister of truth—portrayed in First Book—your fashionable residence —touching the silvery strings of the harp with an easy and cautious hand—but in the coming work—it is then to be spread through the wide spread world, when at present there is not more in circulation, than one half hundred, and those in the hands of men—now residing in city.

But my object in addressing your Ladyship at this Junction, is through many wishes of your companions—men whom I am conversant with—that I should at once—so do.

My dear madam—addressing you upon this delicate point—allow me to say—that if there is a person in this dignified world, who knows your public and private character for the last 14 years—truly it is myself.

My intentions are strong—mighty—fixed. I have visited your residence—many and many a time, and more so, during the last 8 months. I propose to know this day, although I regret on your behalf—that you have been the means of destroying a certain number of females—that I know their origin—your present number of girls or in other words Misses--their names and where they came from, previous to this—their destination.

Also I have now ready for the press volume 2nd and so up to 10, which is all the remaining 9—in each I have impartially portrayed and devoted 30 pages, referring to your character and house, with inmates and scenes.

Now it is my utmost intention—to bring your countless deeds —your "hell of infamy" to rights, and it must be done. One volume counting some 59 pages all upon your past life and enacments, and lately I have visited ———, and their—their I received information, sufficiently replete for one or more entire volumes.

I might speak of many a circumstance now, which would cause the blush and tear—but those Future Pages will speak, without fear, for themselves. My next Volume portrays your manner of living day the day—in short scenes appalling—far more severe than No — —your neighbor.

Many a chick has strived the utmost to suppress it—but it is of no use.

. That club has offered to myself the small sum of $12,000 to suppres it—but those 10 volume I am ready to suppres—the extra work anounced by June, for the sum of $25,000—as this shall be my reward.

It is a work which demands a terrible circulation, and I have spaired no pains in painting your deeds—also I have taken a sketch of your sober features—which work will bear a most natural likeness of your Ladyship.

But I have promised many a Gent, who is acquainted with you, that I would write you, that you might propose, and so I have done.

Now all I can say, is to you, that privately between us for your sake—your exposure and those within and without—I will agree to consume all, relating to you and yours in the remaining 9 volume, and in the coming out next week—even the Legend regarding you, and all—for the small sum of $1000.

Your are making your thousands, you have already made your tens of thousands, and if I proceed I shall stop your house —arrest all things, and herald to the world your life and character.

I will allow you untill Saturday evening—(to morrow) to report by Note your desire, which in or against favor—will be kept on my part from all eyes and observers—this you may not fear.

I have said to our Letter Carrier—to stop at your residence on Saturday afternoon for answer.

Dear Madam—I urge surely not in the least—this subject, but I have in your behalf stated what is soon to be done.

Yours with Respect,

Dear Madam, I have the Honor,

To Be Yours in Haste.

HARRISON GRAY BUCHANAN.

New York City.

May, 1848.

N. B. For security—we give you a certificate preparatory to that effect signed by myself.   H. G. B.

To   *Monday Eve*

Mrs

—— ——

Dear Madam

Doubtless by this period of time, intently you have perused my obliging Note of Saturday last, addressed to your Ladyship, which unswerved communication, I defered untill to day.

Through our Eastern towns and citys—our Southern and Western ones like wise—an overwhelming demand remains ardently for my Work styled " Asmodius or Legends of New York." The First Number spreads its truthful light this week, and my 2d Number, will in a few short days appear.

But my remarks in Note previously sent—you have perused, and I hope you have not regarded that Letter as vain and nugatory—as sent by some vagabond or conspirator—but from my own personage the pen of the Author. Should you deny same— then I pray you rest quiet, and see if my Second Number will not say *striking truth*—yea that I have extended to your Ladyship proposals, but they have been rejected, I urge nothing— standing as I to-day trust, with a character free from terpitude or reproach—as a person rich in the worlds store—I say again —nothing do I urge.

Before me lays now some fifteen Letters from men and women, praying—imploring that their guilt and deviltry—may not be revealed to a most dignified world—but all this is in vain.

My urgent reason in addressing you the other day, was by a vow—that vow in behalf of some fashionable gents whom you know, and yourself like wise, and on your behalf—though then, by note I have extended this slight mark of respect—you knowing that a true—mighty—and terrible exposure regarding you and yours—would be but meek Justice, in the sacred scales of impartial Justice. In obtaining these things, I myself have during 15 months past—paid you over the small sum of $800—that I might partake and find out what I intended previous to Publication.

As I have said before, I intend to put forth your character, in its true light—knowing the harp strings to touch.

During a visit one evening in February, at your residence, I was accompanied by a young Artist, expressly for a sole purpose, and this I had by him—your impartial ministration—that natural sober feature, daguerreotype will accompany this this work, having been executed on wood, some 6 weeks ago.

In my previous Note I remarked that an answer would be called for, on Saturday last, but having a heavy burden of writing to dispose off, I now take the liberty to say—that I urge nothing—for the 200 pages which is devoted to your character and accompanied by Plate, to me in publication, is worth in its end $5000 least.

But if my offer is accepted, then much time—money will be and must, be spent, in obtaining proofs and Facts to fill up those vacant pages.

That offer, which I made you, if accepted will be understood, to remain *mute* on your and my part, and to secure you from intrigue—a certificate from me signed by others, will in its manner, show for itself, that if I should expose you—you can seek redress and portray my vows. If accepted for the behalf of others and off all—not one word shall be said regarding man or woman—found or seen within your number—all shall be drowned or remain silent.

The slight offer which I have made you, could not by me be accepted in no way, from either Miss—— —— — or The —— —— ——. Many a saddening tale can be told, and in one instance, which will cause them to stand before the bar of yonder Halls of Justice—the injury to a person, which person is to me a relative, and the Truth shall be told. You can lay this if you choose before the many " upper-ten" who oft visits you and your verdict may be made in accordance to your wishes. Thousands and tens of thousands lay at my threshhold, for the suppression of Truth, but standing as I do to-day—wealthy in the worlds store, I feel it a duty incumbent upon me—to portray what I must and what I shall, let the blush, and tear fall where it may.

Should I receive no definite answer by Note, through the Post Office addressed me, in my name—*New York City*, by Wednesday Eve—to morrow—I shall then regard it as a duplicate to go on, and certainly on Thursday Morning—that sec-

ond volume, will be placed in the Proof Writers hands—ready
for the type and press.

This is a stated time which I have marked for *all* communications, and I hope it will be understood, that what has been
said, that I mean.

Certainly I have a personal regard for your destiny—but what
I have gathered—all has cost an enormous sum.

You will please regard my sentiments in a truthful manner—
stay all tides of prejudice, concerning this exposure.

Should you intend to accept of same, I will prepare a certificate—send same, and have it all understood by that duplicate.
you will bethink, and judge, in accordance to your many desires.

Madam I remain Yours

New York City

HARRISON GRAY BUCHANAN.

What does this " vagabond and conspirator" mean? In two
places in this letter he says that he is " rich in this world's store,"
and *wealthy*, yet he *begs* for *one thousand dollars* as pay for hiding that which he says it is his *duty* to expose. In another letter
which we have seen, addressed to a respectable and wealthy
firm of gentlmen, who have deposited their letter with the others
in the hands of the Authorities, the vagabond says he is *poor*,
and gives that as his reason for demanding " black mail."

He says in a portion of his work that he is not " a trafficker"
in sin, &c., yet in the above letter he tells the person to whom
he writes that in 15 months he *has* spent *three hundred dollars*
in her " hell of infamy." His personage has been a very good
customer to her " Ladyship," paying $20 per month, according
to his own account. He says that he *has* been a *partaker* and
has learned his lessons from *experience*, and it appears that one
of his relatives has had a hand in the pie, and *suffered* some.
This is the man who is free from " terpitude and reproach;"
this is the thing who talks of his *Divine Master ;* and this *wealthy*
man is the same one who asked a " small compensation" for his
information offered us in the letter signed H. G. Brady, which
we publish on our 109th page, the original of which we offer
for exhibition, and which has been carefully compared with
those signed *Harrison Gray Buchanan*, and found to be from
the same person. In all the letters which he has written de-

manding black mail, which have been placed in the hands of the proper authorities, his demands amount to about $100,000. This is cutting it *rather* fat for a man already "*rich in this world's stores !*"

And yet he says :

"*We write not merely for idle talk, but for the understanding of all—from a desire to do good—to promote the ends of Truth, Justice, Equity, Humanity and Right.*"

What a false-tongued wretch! Why did he not say—"we write for *money*—we would make devils look like angels for ' a lump of gold,' if we only knew how."

We should not have paid this fellow so much attention had not he or some of his vile and mercenary agents bruited around that *we* were the author of his anonymous, libellous and obscene work. We do not covet the *honor*—his style is altogether too *original* for us. He has most signally failed in his attempts to extort money, for his letters have all been placed in the hands of vigilant officers of the law, who it is to be hoped will find the individual, and provide suitable lodgings for him. We are aware that in giving him this lengthy notice we are only advertising his pamphlet, but as it is too vulgar and obscene to be permitted in a decent family—few of *our* readers will care to peruse it. The Police Gazette says :

"Its strictures are perfectly harmless, and should give no more concern to those to whom they allude, than the buzzing of a fly."

Perhaps the Gazette is right—but it ought to show up this fellow's villainous attempts at getting "black-mail," and if we judge rightly of the honesty and independence of its editors, they will give him " a small lift." It will do at any rate as an advertisement, and perhaps aid him in getting that " small compensation," which he so modestly desires. Our greatest cause of anger is that he has attempted to *praise* us in some parts of his work, and we are determined to sue him for libel for the same if he or his publishers can be found ; on the principle, that " if a villain's *slander* is an honest man's *praise*," a villain's *praise* must be an honest man's *slander*.

We have made allusions in several places in our work to the neglect of the Police in suppressing gambling, &c. Upon taking considerable pains to investigate the matter, we find that the fault lays at a *higher* source.

Time after time the police have arrested gamblers, policy-dealers, and other criminals of that kind; and though the offences of these persons were of a nature which makes the penalty a much larger fine, and *one year's* imprisonment, the *courts* have let them off with fines of $25, $50, or $100.

When Mr. Pat Hearn, and Mr. Berry were arrested and fined $100 only, *without imprisonment*, others were also arrested for keeping gambling-houses, who were discharged *without punishment*. And this was done by the "*Court of Special Sessions*," of this city, consisting of the Recorder assisted by two Aldermen.

If these gamblers had been accommodated with a year in the penitentiary, and a few more of their gang served the same way, the gambling-houses would soon "suspend business." We are now satisfied that it is *not* the fault of the police, but of those *negligent and culpable* magistrates who will not punish criminals according to law, when they are arrested. What is a fine of $100, to Pat Hearn? He wins, at an average, ten times the amount every night—sometimes twenty and thirty times the sum, and if he had not others to share it with, would soon be able to "retire from buisness."

If the magistrates will not support and countenance the *arrests* of the police, the latter should not be blamed, but the *former* should be held up to condemnation and shame. We believe they are *sworn* to do their *duty* strictly. They are paid large salaries for doing it, and those salaries are gathered from taxes paid by citizens, who are bound to be protected by these magistrates. If they *neglect* their duties, they leave their characters open to the darkest and most dishonoring inferences.

We shall have the honor of appearing before the public on the fifteenth of July ensuing, with a large Newspaper, under the title of

"NED BUNTLINE'S OWN,"

and in its columns we shall resume this subject, and also examine other city abuses.*   In the mean time we shall not be idle, as the works already alluded to by us on the page before the Appendix will prove.

.We meet in a few days again, reader, therefore we will only say, *au revoir*.

* In anything that we have said regarding the negligence and culpability of the city authorities, we have not meant to reflect against the *present* Mayor. He has taken his station lately, since we commenced this No. of our work, but he has already commenced the work of reform, honestly, firmly and fearlessly. God speed and aid him in his arduous labors—for he has indeed a rough row to hoe. But with the aid of a police which *must* be vigilant, a man whose sense of duty is so strong, whose character is so firm and fearless, cannot fail to produce great and good changes during his administration.

We speak thus without prejudice for or against him or his predecessor—we do not belong to any *party*, we have never given a vote for any man or office, therefore we can well afford to speak independently, especially as we have never spoken to Mr. Havemeyer, and have never exchanged but two letters with him, and these were calling his attention to matters which he has already nobly commenced to reform. Let him continue his work, and let the *courts* do their *duty*, and New York will soon be the proudest and purest specimen of a Republican City in the world, one which can be pointed out as a bright example to the cities of the old world, which now are so fast becoming republicanised. In the language of *Dow, Jr.*, that true philosopher, "*so mote it be !*"

THE END.

www.ingramcontent.com/pod-product-compliance
Lightning Source LLC
LaVergne TN
LVHW081346060426
835508LV00017B/1443